FROM *SUNDAY TIMES* BESTSELLING A

DR RAN

HOW TO BE A BOY

AND DO IT YOUR OWN WAY!

Illustrated by DAVID O'CONNELL

wren & rook

For Rohan, Sajjan, Veer and Oscar

First published in Great Britain in 2023 by Wren & Rook

Text copyright © Dr Ranj Singh 2023
Illustration copyright © David O'Connell 2023
All rights reserved.

The right of Dr Ranj Singh and David O'Connell to be identified as the
author and illustrator respectively of this Work has been asserted by them in
accordance with the Copyright, Designs & Patents Act 1988.

ISBN: 978 1 5263 6496 8

1 3 5 7 9 10 8 6 4 2

MIX
Paper from
responsible sources
FSC
www.fsc.org
FSC® C104740

Wren & Rook
An imprint of
Hachette Children's Group
Part of Hodder & Stoughton
Carmelite House
50 Victoria Embankment
London EC4Y 0DZ

An Hachette UK Company
www.hachette.co.uk
www.hachettechildrens.co.uk

Printed in Italy

The website addresses (URLs) included in this book were valid at the time of going
to press. However, it is possible that contents or addresses may have changed since
the publication of this book. No responsibility for any such changes can be accepted by
either the author or the publisher.

CONTENTS

Introduction	Do I Measure Up?	4
Chapter 1	The M Word	10
Chapter 2	We All Need Allies	38
Chapter 3	Will Boys Be Boys?	80
Chapter 4	Love the Skin You're In	106
Chapter 5	Breaking Down Barriers	128
Conclusion	The Complete You	148
Resources		156
Index		157
Acknowledgements		160

DO I MEASURE UP?

Have you ever asked yourself what 'being a man' really means? It's something I've wondered throughout my life. I always hear people say things like 'man up' or 'boys will be boys', but what are they actually talking about? Do they think that being a boy or a man means that you have to look a certain way or be good at specific things? Can you only be a man if you behave a certain way?

What do **YOU** think?

We're not the only people to have pondered it. In fact, it's a question that has crossed the minds of some of history's greatest thinkers. For example, Albert Einstein was a pretty clever person, right? He possessed possibly the finest scientific mind that humanity has ever seen. His theories and calculations advanced our understanding of physics, the universe and pretty much everything in it. But guess what else he spent time thinking about?

'TRY NOT TO BECOME A MAN OF SUCCESS, BUT RATHER TRY TO BECOME A MAN OF VALUE.'

Clearly, this is a subject that even world-famous scientists have grappled with!

If I had a penny for all the times I sat down when I was younger and wondered if I was 'boy' enough, I'd be rich. OK, maybe not rich, but I'd have more money to spend on cool stuff for sure. Because I didn't always like the same things (like football or Formula 1) that other boys in my class did. I wasn't the one being chosen to be a team captain. Actually, I was usually picked last because I wasn't that good at sports. And often, I felt like there must be something wrong with me.

I know now that all this worry about how to be a boy is **SO** unnecessary because you are who you are – and that's perfectly fine! The thing is, all of us – no matter how boyish or manly we might (or might not) seem – have questioned ourselves and wondered whether we are how we should be. So whatever your reason for picking up this book, I'm going to explore all this with you, and together we'll come up with some answers for those questions in your head. Who knows, you might even be surprised at what you'll find out!

Why all the fuss?

If people have been talking about this stuff for ages, why did I decide to write this book now? For two reasons, really. First, because the subject of how boys or men should be is being spoken about more and more, in all sorts of places. You may have come across discussions about it on TV, at school or on social media. There are lots of opinions around, which is why it's important to learn about it and make up your own mind.

Secondly, we're also hearing a lot about men who aren't behaving well, who attack or hurt others verbally and physically. Sometimes people say this is caused by problems with 'toxic masculinity'. You might think you know what 'masculinity' means – that it describes how a man or a boy ought to be. And yet when people talk about masculinity, it's often because something bad has happened. And that can make it seem like 'masculinity' is a bad word.

DOES THAT MEAN IT'S BAD TO BE MASCULINE?

Definitely not! There are loads of brilliant things about masculinity, if we can only adjust our thinking a bit. And the other thing to note is that not all boys or men *are* masculine (nor do they have to be) – at least not in the traditional sense.

Right now, as you're growing up, is the most important time to be talking about this. This crucial, magical time of life as a boy shapes the kind of man (or person) you'll become. This book will help you go on to become an amazing adult by encouraging you to reflect on what it takes to be kind, good and responsible in today's world. For too long, boys have been left to work it out for themselves. Now you don't have to!

The journey begins here

Right now, the most important thing for us to get our heads around is this: no matter what you might have been told, the first step to being a great boy or man is being whoever you are and respecting yourself. This book is going to pick all your insecurities about 'being a man' apart and show you why they don't need to stress you out.

We'll discover why masculinity isn't about living up to any particular ideal of a man that's set in stone. I want to show you that masculinity can take many different forms – and, above all, be positive. It can be something that we nurture, celebrate and promote in all its shapes and forms.

Take it from me: I've gone from being a boy who pretended to like football because all my friends did, to a teenager who felt that he was too sensitive and emotional to be a 'lad', to a man who is proud to say that he likes fancy dress, enjoys dancing and loves to wear sparkly things. In my forty (ish) years on this planet, I've learned so much about what being a boy or a man *really* means.

We're going to break down what being a boy is and help you work out who you truly are and how to be the best you can be, in your own way, no matter what that is. Think of it as a personal companion teaching you about yourself, guiding you through the challenges of life and encouraging you to always think and act in positive ways – like an antidote to so-called toxic masculinity. I'll show you that the key to it all is as simple as a bit of kindness – to yourself and others. I've also asked some inspirational friends of mine to give you some of their ideas and advice. And I've shone a spotlight on incredible people doing awesome things in the world.

So, why should you read this book? Because it's absolutely **AMAZING** and is going to change your life, of course! Well, I hope it will. Even if it doesn't, it will give your confidence a massive boost. Also, it's going to make you think long and hard about who you are, how you feel and how you express yourself. You don't have to do it all at once. Take one chapter at a time and have a think after each one. Together, we're going to smash down barriers and start thinking about who we really are and who we want to be.

LET'S **DIG IN.**

THE M WORD

1

We're going to start with what we define as masculinity and why. If you picked up the *Oxford English Dictionary* and looked up the word masculinity, it would say: 'qualities regarded as characteristic of men'. But what do we actually mean by that?

Let's begin with a couple of challenges. First, grab a bit of paper and write down which of the following qualities you would associate with being a boy or man. Go on, I'll wait.

Leader   Artistic   Focused   Brave   Musical

Assertive   Creative   Camp   Beautiful

Caring   Protective   Ambitious   Rugged

Tender

Gentle   Strong   Intelligent

Kind

Professional   Funny   Macho

Laddish

Emotional   Understanding   Ally

The 'masculinity scale'

Next, I want you to draw a horizontal line in the middle of a landscape piece of paper. Write 0 at the left end of the line, and 10 at the other end. This is our 'masculinity scale'. Now take all the qualities from the last page and place them somewhere along this scale depending on how masculine you *think* they are (0 for least masculine, 10 for most masculine). Here's an example of what I mean:

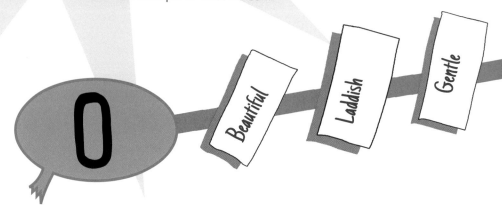

Here's the thing: there is actually no right or wrong answer here, instead it's designed to make you think. It's just a fun way to explore what we define as masculine and why. For example, it shows you that there are many different words to describe masculinity, and that not everyone would use the same words. And you might decide that certain words are more masculine than others, but someone else would put them in a completely different order. Whichever order you chose, remember this: **ALL** of these words can be used when talking about what masculinity is.

So you can be a boy/man and be **ANY** of these things we listed. Likewise, you don't have to be a boy or man to be these things – plenty of girls and women have these attributes too!

Macho

Caring

Rugged

10

Now have another think about your answer to the first question I asked . . . did the qualities you chose remind you of any particular people? And consider the boys and men that you know – what qualities do those people have? When you start thinking about it, you'll find that everyone is different and has different characteristics.

That's the point here: masculinity is not a fixed or set thing, and it isn't the same for everyone. It varies depending on who and what you are talking about. And it is so much more than what society tells us it should be. Yes, we're going to turn everything you might have thought about masculinity on its head!

A brief history of masculinity

At this point, you're probably thinking,

HANG ON, RANJ, YOU CAN'T JUST MAKE UP WHAT BEING A BOY OR MAN IS!

Well, that's exactly what humans have done over time.

Let's start at the very beginning. The Neanderthals were an ancient evolutionary relative of modern-day humans, who walked the Earth until about forty thousand years ago. Look them up in a textbook or online and you'll see a typical picture: the male is usually carrying some sort of tool or weapon and is portrayed as a bit of a brute, while the female is looking after a child and is depicted as the more nurturing one. Even to this day people will use the word Neanderthal to describe thuggish behaviour in boys or men. But are we right to?

We've long assumed that Neanderthals had different roles or jobs because of their biological sex, i.e. how they were born (their genetics). We've always thought that those jobs were determined by some of their physical and behavioural characteristics: men being the hunters and women being the gatherers. However, we've changed our understanding of what they actually did by looking at fossils of their teeth.

How? Well, Neanderthals used their mouths and teeth like a third hand, and looking at the pattern of wear and tear on them shows that they used their mouths for lots of different tasks! Even though you usually see the males characterised as the hunters in popular culture, the fossils suggest that the two genders shared a lot of the same activities, and women might have hunted just as much as the men. So the so-called 'masculine behaviours' were definitely not restricted just to the men.

Now let's fast-forward tens of thousands of years to Sparta, where the roles performed by boys and girls changed again. Sparta was home to an ancient Greek warrior society which became the dominant force in Greece in around 400 BCE. Spartans are often depicted as tough, athletic and muscular warriors. All healthy male children would enter a regime of military education from the age of seven. This encouraged bravery, endurance, self-control and obedience. Once they grew up, they were expected to fight to protect their country. So far, so macho. However, Spartan men were really in touch with their emotions – nobody would have blinked at a man crying in those times. And while girls weren't required to undergo military training, they were educated and, once they grew up, they were in charge of managing land and property. So, while women weren't expected to fight, they were leaders and held authority and power within society. This is interesting, right?

By the time we arrive at the era of the Roman Empire (from around 27 BCE to 476 CE), we find a very different society. Human beings had evolved a long way from our prehistoric ancestors, and their ideas about what it meant to be a man had changed too. Now men were leaders, politicians, doctors and heads of the military (among other things), while women were mainly wives or mothers. The balance of power had men firmly in charge.

Let's jump ahead several hundred years again to the Victorian era, roughly in the 1800s. By this point, the roles of men and women, and the qualities they were expected to have, were clearly defined and pretty much in opposition to one another. Boys and men were to be strong leaders and fighters who didn't show or talk about their emotions. Girls were expected to be quiet and dainty, preparing them for growing into women who took care of the household and the children.

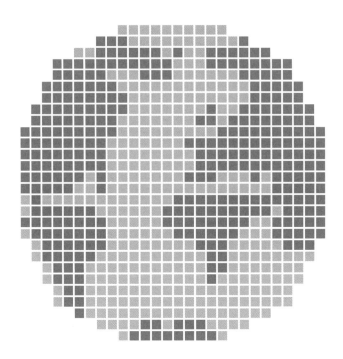

Masculinity across the world

That's a brief history of what it was like to be a boy or man in Western society. However, that's just part of the picture – after all, we don't all live in the West! Different cultures across the world had their own ideas around manhood and masculinity. Let's take a look at some of them . . .

In ancient India (where my ancestors lived), men and women had specific duties like in other places, but the rules around gender were less strict. Their society had a third gender, called **HIJRA**. My ancestors recognised that people could be male, female or something else. The people who made up this third gender were usually born male, but dressed in traditionally feminine ways and had their own duties such as being spiritual or religious figures.

You can see this more open understanding of gender in other parts of Indian culture too. Ancient Indians also recognised that men and women shared attributes. Take a look at Hindu religion and mythology and you'll find figures, gods and goddesses that show both 'male' and 'female' characteristics! In some sections of Hinduism, the god Shiva is shown and described with both male and female attributes.

I know it's getting a bit more complicated here, and we'll explore what we mean by gender a bit later. But ancient India isn't the only place where the idea of other genders, or men and women sharing characteristics, came about.

Many indigenous communities in North America recognise people as more than just male and female too. In fact, some of these cultures have at least four genders (feminine female, masculine female, feminine male and masculine male). These people have believed for centuries that boys and men can have both traditionally male and female qualities — something they also call 'two spirit'.

Modern-day masculinity

OK, you're probably wondering how all this ties in to what masculinity and being a boy means. We've seen from our speedy tour of history that boys were often automatically expected to take on certain roles just because they were boys — like being more physical or being in charge. And it was the same for girls too, who were supposed to be the caring ones. Many people still think like that today. These are what we call gender stereotypes — an automatic belief or over-simplification about someone being a certain way based on their gender, which isn't always true.

Gender stereotypes evolve and become hardened throughout history. They come about because people in charge decide

what they are, or because these beliefs persist for a long enough period of time that people automatically assume they are true. That's why the Victorians were so much more rigid about roles for men and women than the Neanderthals were. Whilst they may help some people work out who they are, they're not always great – gender stereotypes can unfairly label people, limit what they can do and make them feel inadequate if they don't measure up.

THANKS, HISTORY.

But here's the other thing we could choose to take away from the history lesson. Different times, cultures and places have had varying ideas of what masculinity means, which goes to show that as a concept, it isn't fixed – and that's key. History shows us that, far from having to remain rooted to one consistent interpretation of masculinity, we can be free in how we define men and boys. After all, as we go into the future, it's just going to keep on changing.

Let's take a look at current times. Nowadays, we have a range of male role models that young boys can look up to. For example: Justin Trudeau, the prime minister of Canada; actor Idris Elba; Olympians like Sir Mo Farah; dancer and choreographer Yanis Marshall; fashion designers like Kaushik Velendra and Sabyasachi Mukherjee; and pop stars such as Harry Styles and BTS. Each of these people shows us a different type of masculinity. None of them are exactly the same, but all of them are awesome!

MAN OF THE MOMENT: BARACK OBAMA

Barack Obama was the 44th president of the United States and the first ever Black person to hold that title. He already had a pretty impressive political career behind him, having campaigned for things like helping more Black Americans to vote. He believes in peace, equality and fair treatment for all. He is also never afraid to express his emotional side, whether that's his love for his family or crying during press conferences after some of the tragic school shootings that have happened across the United States. One of my favourite quotes from him is: 'When all Americans are treated as equal, no matter who they are or whom they love, we are all more free.' And that's what a good leader should be all about.

In the future, our ideas around masculinity may be completely different again. I'm hopeful that with time we'll be more open to accepting different forms of masculinity. Take our masculinity scale from earlier. One hundred years ago, society wouldn't have associated the word 'emotional' with boys and men. Yet today, more and more people recognise that being aware and in touch with your emotions (something we call emotional intelligence) is important for everyone.

I like to think that we are starting to look at masculinity in a much more inclusive way now, and that's really exciting! But displays of toxic masculinity in our culture, like sexism, aggressive behaviour towards others (such as at sports matches) and violence towards women, prove that we have so much still to do. If we're going to change for the better, we need to take a hard look at what we think of and expect from boys.

THE THING IS, BOYS ARE CAPABLE OF SO MUCH MORE THAN JUST BEING MACHO. AND EXPLAINING THAT TAKES US RIGHT BACK TO OUR UNDERSTANDING OF WHAT GENDER IS.

Gender vs. sex vs. masculinity

Much of how we define masculinity is based on gender: people say that boys have certain traits that make them masculine and girls have certain ones that make them feminine. But it isn't as simple as that. We know that boys and girls can share traits, so masculinity and femininity aren't black and white – and history and other cultures teach us that gender isn't quite so clear-cut either.

When we use the word 'gender', we are usually talking about whether someone is a boy or a girl. We sometimes also use the word 'sex' to describe the same thing (although sex can mean sexual intercourse as well). However, they aren't quite the same thing. It can be tricky to explain the difference between gender and sex, and different people have different perspectives on this, but I like to describe it using a bit of science.

'Sex' can be used to describe what someone is biologically – their biological sex or how someone was born. If you've been paying attention in science class, you'll know that your DNA determines all that you are physically. Everything from the colour of your eyes and hair to how tall you are and the size of your feet. DNA is a set of instructions for making a person.

However, just because someone is born a certain way doesn't mean that they *feel* that way too. Humans are much more complicated than a set of instructions. This is where GENDER IDENTITY comes in. That's why some people use the word gender to describe how they feel and who they are, but biological sex (or 'sex assigned at birth') to describe what they were born as. Most people's biological sex and gender identity are the same. We call this **CISGENDER** (or **CIS**). But there are a small proportion of people for whom they are not the same. They might have been born biologically as a male, but now feel and identify as a girl. The same goes the other way round too. This is what we call **TRANSGENDER** (or **TRANS**).

There are also some people who don't identify as a boy or a girl, but who may be something in between (called gender non-binary), and those who identify as bits of both (known as gender fluid). This might all seem a bit complicated, but it's actually nothing new. We already know from global history that having more than two genders is common in lots of cultures (such as that of indigenous Americans and ancient India).

Gender identity is made up of more than a set of DNA instructions. It's how you feel, what you look like, how you behave, what you like or dislike, all added up to make a more complete picture of you. Getting your head around it all can take a bit of time. You might already know who you are and that's great. But if you don't feel like you have it all worked out yet, don't worry. You're probably not the only one. You don't have to make any decisions until you are ready. As long as you respect each and every person for who they are, you can take all the time you need to learn about it.

BEING A TRANS MAN
JAKE GRAF _ _ _ _ ▮

Jake Graf is an awesome actor, director, screenwriter and transgender rights activist. Here he tells us about being a trans man and the message he'd like to pass on to young people today.

I was brought up as a little girl in the 1980s, so I was raised a certain way – to look pretty and wear dresses. I was made to feel like what I wanted to do and achieve in my life wasn't as important as it was for my cousin (who was a boy). It was the same for so many others that were brought up female in those times.

When I was twenty-eight and began my transition (from woman to man), and started looking and sounding like a man, all of that changed. All of a sudden, the world around me treated me differently: they made space for me and started listening to my opinion more.

As a man, I was expected to be a lot more confident – certainly more than I actually am! I feel very comfortable in my skin now. I finally like the reflection

I see in the mirror. But I feel like I was never taught all of those things that boys are told to build their confidence, such as stand up, be heard and be counted. I wish I hadn't missed out on that.

Life now feels very good, though – like how it was supposed to be. This is the way I have always felt since I was born . . . and I knew from the age of two or three. It's not a choice. It's just who you are and there is absolutely nothing wrong with it. There are lots of different ways to be trans, just like anything else in life, and they are all wonderful.

If you are trans or think you might be, don't worry, don't be scared, because there are many more of us coming out these days and you will find your tribe and the people who love you. I know the world can seem scary sometimes for anyone that is different, but just remember there are lots of good people out there and there is help if you need it. There are people who will love you for who you are.

And for those people who might have a trans friend and are wondering, just remember that they are the same as you. We just have a few things that we need to be realigned for us to be ourselves. We are just the same as anyone else and we deserve the same love, care, respect and place in the world.

> *We shouldn't expect boys and girls, or anyone, to be certain ways. We should let everyone be the best versions of themselves no matter who they are. They should do what they want to do and carve their own path; they should be unafraid to show their difference; they should stand up against wrong; and they should not be scared to show their emotions. We should all show compassion, care and kindness, and try to listen to and have empathy for others. That's not specific to just boys and men – it's for everyone.*

Identity and race

Now let's explore identity in another sense. We can't talk about identity without talking about race and culture, because these things also have a massive influence on who we are and what others expect. I come from an Indian background. Even though some of our history shows us to be quite open when it comes to masculinity and gender, many from my background still think boys have to be a particular way.

The same applies to some other cultures, such as people from African, Afro-Caribbean, Caribbean and Arab backgrounds. Boys and men from these communities may be expected to be really macho and traditionally masculine. Anyone that doesn't feel like that might have a really tough time, especially growing up.

If you are someone from a community like this, I know it can be especially difficult to fully be yourself. For some people it might not be safe to be completely themselves as they grow up. Please remember that even though it may not always feel possible within your community, it isn't the same everywhere, and it won't always be like this. You'll find your own community or tribe as you grow up: somewhere where you belong and can 100 per cent be yourself. In the meantime, make sure you are safe and you can always turn to someone you trust, like a teacher, counsellor or a helpline for support.

I grew up in an Asian community where it was harder for anyone who was different because of how other people reacted. I learned that all of us have a part to play in making sure that everyone feels welcome. Let's try to be that change: if you've got a friend or family member going through a tough time with their identity, then be a good person and try to understand and support them. And if you're the one who is struggling, talk to someone, and if it is safe for you to do so, show the world the wonderful person that you are!

Sexuality

So we've talked about identity in terms of gender, sex and masculinity, but how does sexuality fit into all of this? Sexuality is the word we use to describe who you are attracted to sexually (a.k.a. who you fancy). You might feel a bit young for this sort of stuff right now, but it's important to prepare yourself with all the information for the future. That way you'll make better decisions later.

Let's get into it . . . if you are a boy who is attracted to girls, then you might be **HETEROSEXUAL** or 'straight'. If you are a boy who fancies other boys, then you might be **HOMOSEXUAL** or gay. If you are a boy who likes both, then you might be **BISEXUAL**. If you like neither in that way, then you might be **ASEXUAL**. Some people also use the words **QUEER/QUESTIONING**, which means their sexuality isn't quite fixed, but they don't see themselves as heterosexual. Sometimes we bunch all of these groups together and use the term

LGBTQ+

(this stands for lesbian, gay, bisexual, transgender, queer/questioning and others).

There are still people who believe that to be a boy you should be heterosexual. And then there are those who think even that isn't enough. To be a real man you have to be a certain kind of heterosexual: confident, good-looking, popular with the ladies and so on. I think that all of this is nonsense.

Just like how being a boy and being masculine are separate things, your sexuality is a separate thing too. I'm a man, I'm queer and I'm useless at chatting people up! Likewise, some of my friends are queer and don't feel like their gender is 100 per cent any particular thing, and are super-confident in themselves.

Whoever you fancy or fall in love with has no bearing on whether you can call yourself a boy or not, or on your masculinity. It doesn't make you any less of a man if you love someone of the same gender as you. And it doesn't make you any more of a man if you only fancy girls. Look at the rugby player Gareth Thomas: he's gay and over 6 feet of 'pure bloke'. No matter who you love, you are who you are and you are just as important and loved as anyone else!

BEING QUEER AND ASIAN
RYAN LANJI _ _ _ _ ■

Ryan Lanji is a brilliant TV personality, DJ, producer, fashion curator and queer South Asian man. He was also the winner of *The Big Flower Fight* TV show! He fights for queer people to be recognised, particularly those of colour. He tells us what being a queer person of colour means and what he'd like young boys growing up today to know.

Historically, white people have been in charge, controlling the stories we hear and the way we know the world to be. To be a person of colour means you are someone who isn't white. People of colour are people who are from countries like India, Africa, Asia and more, where our culture, upbringing, religion and even the colour of our skin is different and unique. A queer person of colour is someone who identifies as lesbian, gay, bisexual or gender queer and is also someone who is of colour. For example, my name is Ryan Lanji and I am a South Asian gay man, which makes me a queer person of colour.

My identity is important to me because being who you truly are is such a beautiful feeling. If you grow up trying to be what others want you to be, you'll always find you are being only half of yourself – or sometimes not yourself at all. To me, identity means you are exactly who you are inside on the outside as well. You don't have to be anything you don't want to be and should always be what makes you feel amazing. You can identify as your culture, your gender, your orientation or even your style!

I personally don't relate to the phrase 'being a man' because to me it's an outdated way of thinking – that in order to 'be a man' you have to be loud, brave, strong, successful, courageous, etc. These are all the things I encourage in ALL humans and all genders. 'Being a man' is just an outdated way of saying

BE YOURSELF
AND BE AMAZING!

Instead, think of it this way: how can you be a decent human? I would say be kind, be caring, do what is right and always make the choice to unite your community and help each other. That's what being a decent human means to me.

MYTH BUSTER

BEING CAMP MEANS YOU'RE LESS OF A BOY
Urgh! We hear this time and time again: 'Oh, you're so girly!' As if it's a bad thing or makes you less of a boy. That's ridiculous! You could be a guy and be 'feminine' or a girl who is more 'masculine'. So what? What matters is that you're happy as who you are and you're trying to be a good person.

Homophobia, biphobia and transphobia

Even though everyone has a right to be who they are, sadly there are still some people who will say or do bad things or show hate towards those who are not strictly heterosexual or straight. Hate directed against gay people is called **homophobia**. Likewise, hate shown towards bisexual people is **biphobia**, and hate against transgender people is **transphobia**. Even though we live in an increasingly open and understanding world in many ways, these negative ideas still exist and often they are demonstrated by boys and men.

Why is that? Mainly because people fear what they don't understand. It can be a learned behaviour from adults in their lives. Or they are specifically taught that the world should be a certain way and they need to fear LGBTQ+ people because they're different and don't always conform to the stereotypes they expect.

For some it's because they come from super-conservative communities that won't accept LGBTQ+ people because of their beliefs (which may stem from their religion). There are also those who discriminate against them because they make them feel uncomfortable about themselves (often because they may be LGBTQ+ themselves and not quite ready to admit it).

This hate isn't something we are born with – it's something we learn. But you don't have to pick these messages up from society. You can do your own thing. I've always believed that showing someone hate takes so much more effort than showing kindness. Human beings are naturally sociable beings. We want to connect with others. Being hateful is exhausting, but accepting and understanding who people are, and especially showing each other some kindness, can change everything –

and then EVERYONE feels good!

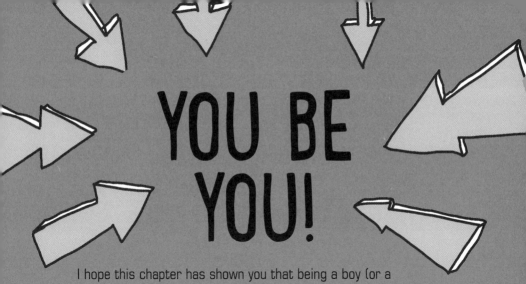

YOU BE YOU!

I hope this chapter has shown you that being a boy (or a man) isn't simply about how you are born. It's also not about behaving a certain way or having particular interests. We need to stop telling ourselves this, because your individual identity is so much more. You can do and be anything you want to be! We are all brilliant human beings who have our own needs, likes and dislikes. We are all wonderfully different and amazingly unique.

Our differences may sometimes set us apart, but they are also what make each one of us special, and they should all be celebrated. Understanding and respecting that being a boy, and masculinity itself, can take many different shapes and forms is part of what being a good person is all about.

Showing love and support to someone who is different to you is something we call **ALLYSHIP**, and we're going to talk about this lots more in the next chapter.

2

Have you ever felt like you needed someone to stand up for you? Perhaps you were being made fun of and it would have felt nice if someone else had your back. Usually it's our friends who step up, and sometimes it's our allies.

You may have heard this term before. For instance, in times of war, allies fight together for the greater good. In this case we're talking about allies as people. An ally is a person who may not have experienced the same difficulty that someone else is going through, but is willing to step up and help in any way that person needs. You've probably already done this for someone: you might have stood up for a girl in your class who was being teased, or you might have protected a person who was being bullied.

This isn't about just supporting your mates, though. Allies are people who care for others and support them because it's the right thing to do, whether they are technically friends with them or not.

AND THERE ARE LOTS OF DIFFERENT WAYS THAT YOU CAN BE AN ALLY.

Being an ally can take lots of different forms:

- Speaking up for someone who is being picked on in the playground (we'll talk more about bullying in the next chapter)

- Speaking out when someone makes a joke about girls (sexism)

- Speaking out when someone makes a joke about LGBTQ+ people (homophobia/biphobia/transphobia)

- Speaking up when someone gets treated differently because of their skin colour (racism)

- Supporting someone who is being bullied, such as letting a teacher or other responsible adult know

- Not teasing girls about their bodies or things like periods

- Not making fun of other boys who like or are into different things

- Checking 'laddish' behaviour when in a group of boys, like breaking up a fight and making sure that no one is hurt

- Checking in with someone after they have had an upsetting event or experience and offering them help

Using your privilege

One thing that allies (especially boys) can use is their privilege. What's that, I hear you ask? Boys (and men) are treated differently simply because of who they are – remember what Jake Graf said about people seeing him differently once he'd transitioned? When you're a boy or a man, society and the world automatically give you certain advantages: you're more likely to be seen and heard, be in a position of power or get a higher-paid job, because society finds it easier to imagine you there thanks to gender stereotypes. For example, most world leaders are male and most company CEOs are male. This isn't because men are better at these jobs, but because they are more likely to get them. This is called **MALE PRIVILEGE** – an automatic advantage based on being male. Even if your family doesn't have much money or you live in a poor part of town, if you are a boy you still have male privilege. Similarly, white people get certain advantages over people of colour purely on the basis of their skin colour – something called **WHITE PRIVILEGE**. There are other types of privilege too, such as **SOCIO-ECONOMIC PRIVILEGE**, which means advantages someone receives if their family has more money and a higher social status than others. All these privileges (and whether someone has them or not) affect how we are treated by others and our experiences in the world.

It can feel really uncomfortable to discover that you have privilege. Some people don't like to think about it because they feel like it suggests they didn't work hard for their achievements.

They probably did – but they will have had a head start over someone with less privilege. So while you may not be able to do anything about being privileged, what you can do is recognise it. That means acknowledging that other people might encounter difficult situations that you never will, and that you might be able to help them. Allyship is one way of using any privilege you have in a positive way, and more and more men (and people) are doing this.

Don't be a bystander!

When you see something happening that isn't right, it's important to speak up if you can. Otherwise, you become a **BYSTANDER** – someone who knows that something is wrong but doesn't do anything about it. For instance, you might hear someone making fun of someone else's appearance. Obviously that's not OK – but if you don't step in, everyone will assume that you're fine with it. And not only does the perpetrator get away with it, they might go on to do it to another person.

By stepping in, you could break that cycle and let the victim know that they are not alone in their situation. What was originally a very negative experience then becomes something that everyone learns from: the perpetrator finds out that their behaviour is not OK and the victim learns that they have support.

Dare to be brave

You'll have noticed that all of these things involve some level of bravery. This doesn't always come easily, but I can definitely tell you that the more you do it, the easier it gets.

I used to be a really shy kid. At school I would often disagree with some of the stuff the other boys did (like if they were pushing someone around), but I didn't always feel brave enough to say anything because I didn't want to become a target too. So instead I'd check on the person afterwards to make sure they were OK. Looking back, I sometimes wish I'd had the courage to say something in the moment – but at least I did what I felt I could at the time. It's important to be brave but also be safe, and to never put yourself in harm's way.

Bravery doesn't mean getting up to fight (although a lot of people think it does). It simply means having the courage to say something is wrong and then doing something about it, even if that makes you feel a bit scared. If you're unsure of when or how to act, take a moment now to learn about it. For example, get involved with anti-bullying groups or check out some of the anti-bullying resources at the end of this book. That way you could know how to spot it and feel more empowered to step in if you see it happening. Go and learn about the LGBTQ+ community (most schools have a diversity week to teach people about this) and speak to LGBTQ+ people about their experiences. What have they found hard and how do they think others could have helped?

Perhaps you could start a petition with others in your school to make sure that homophobic or transphobic language isn't tolerated. Listen to your girl friends' experiences, and if you ever see someone picking on them, just take them to one side and engage them in conversation so that the bully isn't given any attention. And you don't have to do it alone — bravery is easier when we all do it together!

I've been thinking a lot about allyship recently, especially how I can be a better ally to trans people. If you read newspapers or go online, you'll see that trans people are often attacked or vilified, especially on social media. So I've made a conscious effort to actively listen to trans people about how they feel and how they would like to be treated. Like everyone else, trans people deserve to be heard and respected!

R.E.S.P.E.C.T.

Respect is one of my favourite
words. It's also one of my
favourite songs, by the great
Aretha Franklin. She was one of
the greatest Black American soul
singers of all time. She was like
the Beyoncé of her day (in fact, she
inspired Beyoncé). Anyways, I've
gone off topic . . .

Respect is something we show to other people when we are listening to them, and when we acknowledge that they have ideas and opinions too. These may not necessarily be the same ones that we have, but we *respect* their right to have them (just as we do). It's treating others as equals to ourselves. So when you disagree with something your friend might say, you still listen to what they have to say – that's showing respect. When someone comes from a different culture or background to you, and you want to learn about it – that's showing respect. When someone in school wants to wear something that you might not necessarily wear, but you let them live their best life – that's showing respect. And when an adult asks you to listen, and you pay attention – that's showing respect!

IN A SIMILAR WAY, IT'S IMPORTANT TO HAVE SELF-RESPECT.

That means valuing who you are and remembering that you have a voice, feelings and needs just like anyone else, and that they should not be trampled on. You are important as well!

Consent

Respect is also a big part of something called consent. Consent is what you give to someone else when you agree to something. For example, if you need an operation, you or your parent/carer will usually have to give the doctor permission to do it. This is one way of giving consent. Another way is when you're playfighting with your friends (we've all done it). Even if you don't say it explicitly, you've got an agreement with your mates that it's OK, but any of you could stop it by saying so and you would all respect that.

When it comes to consent, you are respecting a person's right to choose and you are respecting their decision, whatever it might be. And you respect that they can change their mind at any time.

There are certain rules around consent: you need to understand what it is you are consenting to (the pros and the cons), the risks of it and what it might mean for you. Plus, you have to be giving your consent freely. Being forced or pressured into agreeing to something is not consent.

One area where this is **REALLY** important is relationships and sex. I appreciate this may be a long way off for you yet (and that's OK because I'm just preparing you for the future), but if and when you decide to do anything intimate with another person, it should always be consensual. When two people do anything that is sexual together, they must both agree to it and be happy doing it. And either of you can change your mind at any time. Listening to and respecting each other's wishes is part of being a responsible adult and a decent person!

IN THE UK
YOU ARE ONLY ABLE TO LEGALLY
CONSENT TO SEX AT THE AGE OF SIXTEEN. THIS
IS CALLED THE AGE OF CONSENT, BECAUSE BEFORE THEN,
YOU ARE NOT YET MATURE ENOUGH TO FULLY CONSENT TO SEXUAL
ACTIVITY - YOU MAY NOT COMPLETELY UNDERSTAND WHAT IT INVOLVES.
REMEMBER, THE LAW IS THERE TO PROTECT YOU AND KEEP YOU SAFE,
NOT TO CRIMINALISE YOUNG PEOPLE. IF YOU STILL DONT FEEL READY AT
SIXTEEN, ITS PERFECTLY OK TO WAIT UNTIL YOURE OLDER.
YOUR BODY IS YOURS AND BELONGS TO YOU ONLY, AND YOU
GET TO DECIDE WHAT HAPPENS TO IT.
IT'S ALL ABOUT RESPECT.

You may be able to consent to other stuff under the age of sixteen, though, such as medical treatment, so long as it is in your best interests and the person treating you (like a doctor or nurse) is confident that you understand everything it involves. If you are unsure, you can always ask an adult to help explain it.

If anyone ever pressurises you into doing something sexual that you don't want to, then it's important to tell a trusted adult straight away. If you don't feel like you can do this, you can also speak to a helpline (like Childline – there are details at the end of the book) or you can call the police if you feel unsafe. Similarly, forcing someone to do anything against their will is not OK, so you should never do it.

Consent and respect don't just apply to sex. Ideally all your interactions with others should be respectful. And if you ever see someone being made to do something or anything being done to them against their will, be brave enough to call it out and make sure the person is OK.

Girls deserve respect

Girls and boys are often treated differently during childhood. That might make you feel like you can't relate to them. You must have seen it: girls are encouraged to play with dolls, play dress-up and learn how to put on make-up, while boys are supposed to play cops and robbers, get into sports or ride bikes. That's not because there is a lot inherently different about them or because of what they can do. If you think that all boys and girls are naturally good at different activities, think again!

At school, you'll see groups of girls and boys hanging out separately. Sometimes that's because they've been conditioned to split off, while others feel safer or more comfortable being with people like themselves who understand what they are going through. But even though we may look different physically, boys and girls are much more alike than you might think.

In fact, the brains of boys and girls are actually quite similar when they're growing up. Mostly, the roles we see are thanks to gender stereotypes and expectations which have been shaped by history and can be unhelpfully constricting.

Even when it comes to puberty – the process when a child's body develops into a more adult body, which is quite different for boys and girls – everyone tends to face similar challenges.

We all grapple with a changing body and how to find our place in the world! I was worried about not being very muscular when I was a kid. My friend was worried about starting her periods. Two totally different experiences, but both of us shared a concern about the development of our bodies. (I'm still not very muscular, by the way. And you know what? I don't care.)

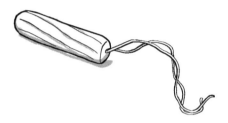

So if a girl you know is going through puberty or any other kind of life event, it's always better to be understanding and to show them respect. If you notice them worrying, perhaps ask, 'Is there anything I can do to help? Do you want to talk about it or would you rather we left the subject alone? Is there anything I can get you?' Because, guess what, you will go through puberty too if you haven't already – and then you'll appreciate the same kindness towards you.

He for she

Wherever you look, it's pretty clear that boys get treated differently to girls (this is the basis of male privilege). For example, girls are judged more harshly when it comes to their appearance and how they behave. There are even people who think that boys and men are better than girls and women just because of their gender. For instance, they say that women can't do certain jobs (like being builders – guess what, they can!) or that they should stay at home and men should work (we all know that's nonsense too!). Women have a harder time finding the same kinds of jobs as men, or even getting paid the same. This is what we call **SEXISM**. It can work the other way too. Men can be discriminated against on the basis of their gender – like people who say that men can't be stay-at-home dads – although this tends to happen much less.

Often, sexism is caused by something called misogyny, which means having an automatic dislike of women and girls or treating them with less respect just because of their gender. It might sound old-fashioned but it still happens today and is something we all need to work to stop. You may not have realised that you're doing it. For example, interrupting or speaking over girls or assuming that you know what their views on something are without actually asking them. Wolf-whistling at girls as they walk past and other kinds of 'laddish' behaviour like it need to become a thing of the past too!

While we have gradually made progress in making things more equal – for example, in the UK, women were finally given the same right to vote as men in 1928 – we can still see sexism and misogyny in everyday life. Part of your job as being the best boy (and man) you can be is not to let it happen. Yes, we're talking about being an ally again: always treating girls as equals and calling out sexist behaviour when you see it. Standing up for the rights of girls and women is called being a **FEMINIST**, and men can be feminists too.

FEMINIST ICONS

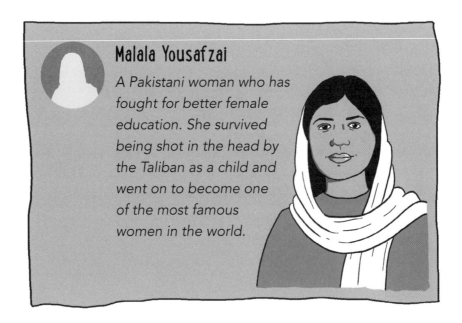

Malala Yousafzai

A Pakistani woman who has fought for better female education. She survived being shot in the head by the Taliban as a child and went on to become one of the most famous women in the world.

Emmeline Pankhurst

An activist from the early twentieth century who fought for women's right to vote in Britain (she was part of a group of women who were termed the suffragettes).

Laverne Cox

A Black American actress who is also a trans woman. She has often spoken publicly about how she was a feminist before she transitioned, and how she is still a feminist now.

Alexandria Ocasio-Cortez

A Latin American politician who became the youngest woman in history to be elected to the US House of Representatives and often speaks up for women's rights.

Feminism is a movement that advocates for women being treated exactly the same as men in all parts of life. This work has been mainly led by women, but men (or anyone) can be feminists too by supporting them in fighting for equal rights. Feminist men are allies to women.

MAN OF THE MOMENT: HARRY STYLES

Harry Styles is an international pop icon who started his career as part of the boy band One Direction. Since then, he's gone on to have an amazing music career of his own, but has also carved out his own identity as a modern man. He often wears gender-neutral clothes (clothes that could be worn by boys or girls) or might be seen sporting a dress (and making it look pretty awesome). He likes nail varnish and mascara, and sometimes carries a purse. He's dated some of the coolest women around, and plenty of guys either want to be him or be like him. But it's his allyship that really stands out and is something he is very proud of. At one of his concerts he said, 'If you are Black, if you are white, if you are gay, if you are straight, if you are transgender – whoever you are, whoever you want to be, I support you. I love every single one of you.' He also believes in feminism, as he said in an interview with Rolling

Stone *magazine: 'Of course men and women should be equal. I don't want a lot of credit for being a feminist. It's pretty simple. I think the ideals of feminism are pretty straightforward.' And for me, that makes him one of the coolest people on the planet right now.*

BEING A MAN (ACCORDING TO A WOMAN)
EMMA MORRIS _ _ _ _ ■

I wanted to get an idea of what being a 'good man' was through the eyes of a woman. After all, women make up half of the global population! So I asked Emma Morris, one of my best friends, what she thought and how every boy could grow up to be their best. Emma is a super-successful TV executive, and someone I always turn to for guidance on life, work, relationships . . . basically everything you would ask a best mate!

Being a woman in a male-dominated world can be exciting, confusing, challenging and sometimes scary . . .

Exciting because we live in a society which increasingly promotes equality (even though we're not completely there yet). Women should have the same social, political and economic rights as men, and nowadays there are laws in place to back up and protect those rights. We've come so far in such a short time – it's not that long ago women couldn't even vote!

It's confusing because it's all there on paper and enshrined in law, but in reality there's still so far to go. Sadly there is still a lot of work to be done to ensure that everyone is completely equal in everything.

It's challenging because there is still a stigma attached to female leaders, there is still an imbalance in women in management roles and there are still too many females being paid less than their male colleagues for doing the same role.

And it's scary because there is still too big a risk to women's safety. I don't know any female friends who'd say they feel safe walking home alone at night. Yet I don't have any male friends who have that worry.

We can start levelling the playing field by making sure that boys and men are better allies to women. First, by calling out the boys and men who contribute to or cause the above. We need to be brave enough to point out the people and attitudes that are the problem. If boys and men started doing that themselves, it would automatically help everyone else. Secondly, it would be even better if everyone was a feminist!

LGBTQ+ allyship

Just as women and girls have it harder than men and boys, people who are LGBTQ+ are also instantly at a disadvantage. In recent years, anti-LGBTQ+ bullying has been the number one form of bullying in UK schools. LGBTQ+ people are more likely to experience mental illness than heterosexual people. Plus, it's actually illegal to be LGBTQ+ in around 70 countries in the world. Doesn't seem fair, does it? Things are slowly changing for the better, but there is still a long way to go.

This could affect you or someone you know or care about. It could be a friend, a member of your family or even someone you know at school. I'm part of the LGBTQ+ community, and while I've not faced direct discrimination myself, friends of mine have been hurt purely for being gay. Why should anyone be discriminated against just because of who they are or who they love?

LGBTQ+ people exist all over the world, in every single country and in every single culture. Here in the UK, we have Pride events which celebrate LGBTQ+ people, as well as initiatives like School Diversity Week, but we still have people who think or behave negatively towards LGBTQ+ people. This is why LGBTQ+ allies are so important – we need people to actively support and speak up for the community, even if they aren't part of it themselves.

SO HOW COULD YOU BE AN LGBTQ+ ALLY? HERE ARE SOME EXAMPLES:

- Educate yourself and learn about LGBTQ+ people and the difficulties they can face in everyday life

- Ask your LGBTQ+ friends about how you could be a better friend to them, and let them know that you have their back and they can talk to you if they need to

- Include LGBTQ+ people who may be feeling left out in everyday things like school activities or sports

- Get involved with events celebrating LGBTQ+ Pride

You're not going to get it right every time, but trust me, trying to be a better ally is an amazing thing and people will forgive you if you make a mistake and own it! If in doubt, just treat others how you would like to be treated yourself.

And if you are LGBTQ+ yourself and you are struggling, remember that you are **EXACTLY** who you are meant to be and you are **AWESOME**. Take it from me: there is nothing wrong with you. In fact, you have something really special: the chance to show the world just how amazingly diverse and wonderful we can be. No one likes living life in black and white. Living it in its full, colourful glory is so much more fun! And if you are battling with who you are, or the way others are treating you, please speak to an adult that you can trust. I promise you that things can and will get better, and you deserve to be just as happy as anyone else.

There are also details of helplines at the end of this book which could be useful too.

BEING THE BEST ALLY YOU CAN BE

SUKI SANDHU _ _ _ _ ■

Suki Sandhu is a bit of an LGBTQ+ legend in the business world. He is the founder and CEO of a recruitment company that finds and places diverse people (gender, race and sexuality) in senior jobs in businesses across the world. Suki wrote a book all about using allyship to create more inclusive workplaces, so I wanted to get his advice on how he thinks boys and young men can be better allies to LGBTQ+ people too.

It's important for everyone to be able to be 100 per cent who they are. In the words of Oscar Wilde, 'Be yourself because everyone else is taken.' You only get to live one life so live it unapologetically as you are. You don't want to regret hiding your identity, personality or emotions later in life. Always try to build bridges with those who may seem against you and if it doesn't work, then let it go and move on. Don't waste your time trying to please others.

It can be even trickier for queer people of colour because lack of visible role models in the past has made them think they're alone. I used to think I was the only gay Indian in the entire world until I went to a social event with lots of people like me there and my mind was blown. I had found my tribe and haven't looked back since.

This is why allyship is so important for everyone in the LGBTQ+ community. If we predict the world is 7 to 10 per cent LGBTQ+ then that means 90 to 93 per cent of the world is straight. The majority has to help the minority for equality and human rights. The LGBTQ+ community cannot do it alone. Allyship shows that you truly care for those who are different to you through actions you undertake, like flying the rainbow flag, donating to LGBTQ+ charities or actively participating in LGBTQ+ events.

Celebrating and championing diversity brings a richness of life and experiences that open your mind and help you to build empathy for others. Without it, life would be grey and boring and unaccepting. The world needs more diversity and inclusion to bring more colour into everyone's lives!

Be an anti-racist

Racism is the word we use when someone treats someone differently (usually in a bad way) just because of the colour of their skin. If you're a person of colour, then you may even have experienced this yourself. Racism is a form of **PREJUDICE** – this means disliking someone for no good reason. And racial prejudice is often used as a reason for bullying.

XENOPHOBIA, another type of prejudice which is similar to racism, is the fear of others because they are from a different country. It is another reason why people discriminate against others because of who they are.

Racism and xenophobia have been around for a very long time and, while in many ways things are better than they used to be, their impact is still felt today.

YOU MAY HAVE HEARD ABOUT

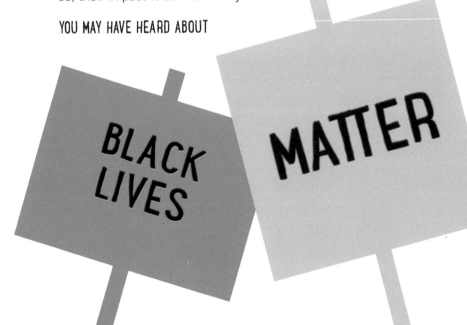

Black Lives Matter (BLM) is a movement that came about because of the way Black Americans are being treated in the USA and the injustice they face every day. Not only does the movement tell people about what is going on, but it encourages them to do something to make things better.

People of other nations and cultures have experienced and still face racism too. When South Asian (such as Indian, Pakistani and Bengali) people first started migrating to the UK in the mid-twentieth century, they were faced with racist taunts, name-calling and being treated like second-class citizens by the majority white population. They are now the biggest ethnic minority group in our country and have contributed so much to British society, but still sadly suffer some of those attitudes today. This will also be familiar to people from East Asia (such as those from China, Japan and Korea) as well.

Conversations around racism have increased, especially after BLM. We are starting to understand that simply not being racist isn't good enough – we have to be actively anti-racist. Here are some examples of what this means.

Non-racist

- Learn about other cultures, backgrounds, religions and parts of the world where customs and traditions might be different

- Speak to people of colour, listen to the difficulties they have faced and try to understand why things might be harder for them

- Avoid making racist comments (like name-calling) or racist behaviours (like treating people of colour differently)

- Don't automatically make assumptions on the basis of culture or skin colour. For example, just because someone wears a hijab, it doesn't mean they're not interested in talking about hairstyles, or just because someone wears a turban, it doesn't mean they can't go swimming. Instead, ask them if they can/would like to!

Anti-racist

- If you hear someone say something racist, call it out. Tell them it's not OK. Asking them to apologise is even better

- Make an effort to include people of colour in activities and your friendship groups

- Recognise that things are often more difficult for people of colour and be an ally to help make things better for them. For example, for your next school project, why not get together people from different backgrounds and all create a noticeboard which depicts anti-racist icons and points out how we can all be anti-racist?

- Be mindful of 'saviourism'. This is where a person acts on behalf of someone else because they think they know better, without actually taking that person's thoughts and feelings into consideration. For example, someone who is white may feel like they need to protect someone of colour, but this may be unnecessary. Instead, they've ended up making the situation about themselves, rather than being there to support the needs of others and focusing on them. As my friend Suki says, if in doubt, ask yourself: *Am I acting because it's the right thing to do and putting others before me, or am I doing this to make myself feel better and make myself look good to those around me? Have I asked the other person what they want me to do?*

ANTI-RACISM ICONS

Colin Kaepernick

An NFL player in the USA who took the knee when the national anthem was played before each game to protest against the unfair treatment of African Americans by the police.

Martin Luther King Jr

An African American civil rights leader who made history by campaigning for better treatment of Black people.

Reni Eddo-Lodge

An award-winning journalist, author and podcaster who wrote the groundbreaking book Why I'm No Longer Talking to White People About Race.

Dr Russell Jeung

An Asian American sociologist who tracked reports of anti-Asian discrimination during the COVID-19 pandemic and set up the Stop AAPI Hate organisation to reduce this type of racism.

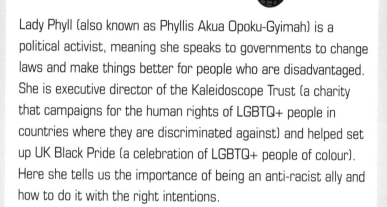

ANTI RACISM ALLYSHIP
LADY PHYLL ____■

Lady Phyll (also known as Phyllis Akua Opoku-Gyimah) is a political activist, meaning she speaks to governments to change laws and make things better for people who are disadvantaged. She is executive director of the Kaleidoscope Trust (a charity that campaigns for the human rights of LGBTQ+ people in countries where they are discriminated against) and helped set up UK Black Pride (a celebration of LGBTQ+ people of colour). Here she tells us the importance of being an anti-racist ally and how to do it with the right intentions.

In terms of being an ally, young people need to know that everyone has a form of privilege somewhere along the line, and it's about how we use it to amplify others. The first thing we should be doing is active listening: listening to those with lived experience of racism, sexism, misogyny and all forms of discrimination, and asking non-combative questions to really take part in the conversation.

Secondly, it's important for allies (especially white people) to make sure that they are doing their research. *There are so many books, podcasts and organisations out there, from Black Minds Matter to UK Black Pride and South Asian Heritage Month. Find out about these organisations – Google is your friend! – to become better informed.*

Thirdly, to avoid the danger of 'saviourism', make sure that you attend events like UK Black Pride, Trans Pride and Bi Pride. Know that you are there as a guest and try to understand why these spaces were created. They're not just for people to have a good time, but ways for us to set the strategy. Understand that these events, which are 'by us and for us', amplify a particular group of people that haven't historically had the same spaces as those in the mainstream.

If you are able to, then donate, support or even volunteer your time or any expertise. You'll find that this opens up your mind further to being clear and transparent about your intentions to do good, and not in a tokenistic way. Your allyship has to be meaningful, regardless of your age, gender, social categorisation or socio-economic status. First and foremost, it has to be real.

Young people, no matter who they are or what their background, are going through a lot right now. But we can all do better at what we do to support each other. Different is good!

MAN OF THE MOMENT: BALWINDER SINGH RANA

Balwinder Singh Rana is a British Indian anti-racism activist who set up the Indian Youth Federation, the very first Indian youth organisation in the UK! He came to the UK from India in 1963 at the age of sixteen and immediately felt the effects of racism from the local people. Since then he has set up numerous anti-racism organisations, including Sikhs Against the English Defence League, has worked for the Anti-Nazi League and has organised marches and protests against racial injustice. He has been a leading figure in the fight against racism for all people of colour, especially South Asians, and continues to do so to this day.

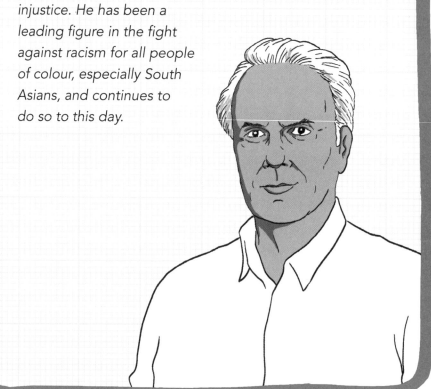

Celebrate difference!

Like all animals, you could argue that we are naturally programmed to be wary of anything different to ourselves because it might be a threat. We automatically fear what we do not understand. We see the same thing happening throughout nature. However, we humans have moved on from that.

We aren't just animals. We are intelligent, understanding, kind and caring individuals!

Fear might be something we are born with, but hate and discrimination are things we learn. Difference is something that we should all respect and celebrate, no matter what it might be: race, religion, gender, sexuality, ability. Not everyone is the same and neither should we have to be. Our differences mean a chance to share new ideas and ways of doing things, and that brings progress.

PLUS, IT MAKES LIFE SO MUCH MORE INTERESTING!

Be the change you want to see

I'm hoping that now you've finished reading this chapter, you have some ideas about how YOU could be a better ally too. Part of being a good person is trying to make things better and more equal for everyone. We can talk and talk about it, but it's our actions that will make a difference. Sometimes we have to be the change that we want to see – and that means being brave enough to do it.

This doesn't always have to be some massively grand gesture. It could also mean doing some research of your own first and then changing your behaviour bit by bit. Perhaps you might like to talk to people about their experiences and learn from them directly (this is always a good idea in my opinion). It can take time and you may make some mistakes along the way, but that's OK. It's the trying that counts and people will appreciate and respect you for it! And don't forget – it's always important that you feel safe in your allyship.

So here's a little exercise for you . . . have a think about someone you may already know and how you could become (or already are) an ally to them. Think of three things you could do today to support them and write them down. Can you use these three things for other people or situations too? And just like that, it becomes easier to see how you can make a difference.

1...2...3...

NOW PUT THEM INTO ACTION!

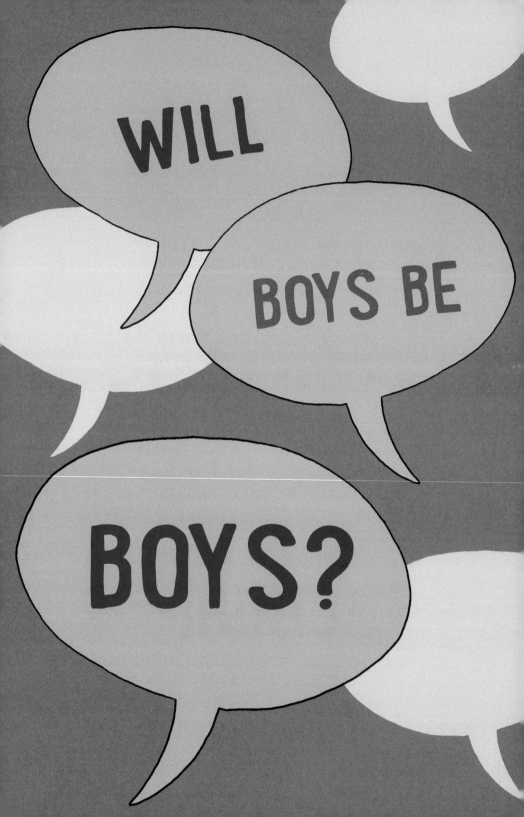

3

Often when boys behave in certain ways, especially when they misbehave, people say 'boys will be boys' as if it's OK. I've always found that a bit odd, because it both justifies bad behaviour and suggests that all boys are like that.

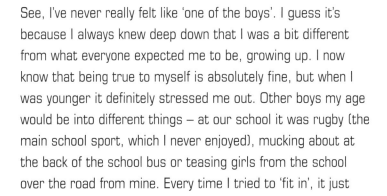

See, I've never really felt like 'one of the boys'. I guess it's because I always knew deep down that I was a bit different from what everyone expected me to be, growing up. I now know that being true to myself is absolutely fine, but when I was younger it definitely stressed me out. Other boys my age would be into different things – at our school it was rugby (the main school sport, which I never enjoyed), mucking about at the back of the school bus or teasing girls from the school over the road from mine. Every time I tried to 'fit in', it just didn't feel like I was being me.

I distinctly remember waiting for the bus home at the end of every school day. As soon as it arrived you'd get a big hoard of people trying to clamber in through the doors. There would always be a bunch of boys at the back who thought it was funny to push everyone forward so they were crushed against the bus. They thought it was hilarious. I thought it was stupid.

At the time I thought it was just people being nasty. But now I understand that it was because they all just wanted to be part of the gang. Some of them were doing it simply because others were. When we're in a group, we can exhibit behaviours that we normally wouldn't, especially bad ones.

We don't always want to do something bad, but the feeling of needing to be part of the group takes over.

And we copy each other or egg each other on because we want to look cool, but it's so easy to get carried away. It might seem fun to you – but it's always worth taking a look around to see who else might be affected by what you're doing.

IS IT FUN FOR EVERYONE?

Don't get me wrong, I wanted to belong to a group at school too. And eventually I found a group of friends who were just like me: a little bit different. And even though we weren't all into the same stuff (my friends Chris, James and Adrian really liked heavy metal music, but I was always more of a pop fan), we still got along just fine. We had our own group. And that made school so much better!

So I guess there are two messages here. First, don't worry if you feel like an outsider or not what others expect you to be. You'll eventually find your tribe and things will feel so much easier. And secondly, you don't have to be like everyone else. In fact, being unique makes you even more special.

You're probably thinking,

That's all well and good, Ranj, but what do I do about it all right now?

Well, if you're having a difficult time with other people at school, you're feeling pressure from your peers or you just want to be a better friend to people around you, then this chapter should help.

Release the pressure

It's nice to be part of the group, to feel popular and to feel like you belong to something. Having a group of friends is a really positive thing because you can enjoy spending time together and support each other when in need. Still, even though you're part of a collective, you can and should be able to be yourself. The best kinds of friends share things they all like together, but also recognise that everyone has their own personalities, interests and needs too.

However, there are times when you might do things to be part of a group that you wouldn't usually. It can feel like you have to behave a certain way just because your friends do or tell you to. This is called **PEER PRESSURE**.

Not sure if you're feeling the pressure? Here are some tell-tale signs or things to look out for:

Feeling like you have to do things just to stay part of the group

Ignoring or allowing behaviour in your friends that you know is bad

Breaking rules because other people in the group are or are asking you to

If you find yourself in this situation, remember that even though the pressure can feel quite full-on, you are still your own person with your own mind. You are responsible for your own actions. You don't have to do something because a friend or someone in your group tells you to – especially if you know it's wrong, hurts another person or might get you into trouble. This is where having some bravery comes in handy again – just like in the section in the last chapter on not being a bystander and using your bravery to be better.

For example, your friends might be teasing someone and it feels like there is an expectation for you to get involved. Deep down you know it's not right and not fair, and it is making someone else feel uncomfortable. Imagine if the person on the receiving end was you. Don't just do the easy thing and join in. Tell your friends that you don't want to do it and check the other person is OK. Trust me, you'll feel so much better about yourself in the long run.

And if that means you can't be part of the group, don't worry. I promise you'll find other friends who respect you for who you are and you'll be much happier. If getting away from peer pressure is hard, then speak to an adult to see if they can help you.

Speaking of respect, let's take a look at some other examples of 'boys being boys' and think about whether they're as harmless as they might first seem.

Wolf-whistling

Whistling is something we all like to do. And it's just a bit of fun,

RIGHT?

Whistling to yourself is one thing, but whistling at someone you don't know as they walk past is another thing entirely. Sadly, it's usually groups of men or boys doing it to women or girls. Unsurprisingly, it can make them feel really uncomfortable or even unsafe, and that is not OK.

Wolf-whistling at someone you know and like, and who you know likes you back? That's fine! Doing it to someone you don't know? Not OK.

And why is it called 'wolf-whistling', you ask? It comes from the whistling sounds shepherds used to warn each other and their dogs if wolves were around. To be honest, I'd take it as a warning sign now too, but in a different way!

Cat-calling

Cat-calling (yes, another animal reference!) is when a person shouts things at someone (usually a girl or woman) on the street. They might shout a compliment, or not-so-nice or even sexual things.

The problem is that even if you think you're saying something nice, cat-calling can make people feel unsafe because they don't know you or your intentions. Just like how we mentioned consent earlier in the book, the person being cat-called hasn't consented to enter into that conversation. They're just minding their own business and going about their day! Lots of my girl friends have had this happen to them and none have said that it was something they welcomed.

So if you like someone that you don't know, perhaps try just introducing yourself first and getting to know them rather than cat-calling. But only if they feel safe and want to chat back!

It's just banter!

You'll have heard this phrase quite a lot, but I'll bet you haven't thought deeply about what it means or how it can make others feel.

Banter is a word we use when we say something insulting but then we make a joke out of it to suggest we don't really mean it. It's done quite a lot just for 'fun', often between groups of people. For example, banter might be used to make fun of the way someone looks (it used to be people with ginger hair when I was growing up), or the way they act (LGBTQ+ people experience this a lot), or because of who they are (girls being called 'birds' for instance).

Usually, people who use banter don't mean any harm. Lots of comedians use it as part of their routine. And some people even use it as a way of flirting. Banter isn't always a bad thing in itself if everyone involved is enjoying the joke.

However, just because the person dishing out the banter doesn't think it's hurtful, doesn't mean that the person on the receiving end feels the same way. And, if the target of the banter takes offence at it, that could make them look like they can't take a joke and it could open them up to even more ridicule. There's nothing worse than being on the receiving end of unkind words and then being made to feel even worse because you spoke up about it.

If you're not sure whether you have that kind of relationship with someone, it's usually best just to avoid it.

That's so gay!

This is a phrase I used to hear a lot at school, and thankfully it doesn't happen as much any more. However, it's NEVER acceptable to say and it's *not* banter. Why do people say it? Well, it comes from the belief that being gay is a bad thing, and so they use it as an insult or to say that something is bad. In the same way that people using horrible words such as 'poof', 'homo' or 'faggot' to hurt people is homophobic, calling something 'gay' in this way is homophobic too.

You sometimes hear LGBTQ+ people using these words themselves (like the word 'queer', which was said as an insult in the past). But that's because the LGBTQ+ community has *reclaimed* the words, giving them a new and joyful meaning. Even so, some will still find these words offensive or hurtful (usually because they were used against them at some point). If you're not from the LGBTQ+ community, then using these sorts of words, especially in a negative way, is not OK.

Don't be a bully

OK, so we've covered banter, where we might unintentionally hurt someone with our words. Now let's go one step further and talk about bullying.

Bullying, after all, doesn't always involve physically hurting someone. Bullying can be anything that belittles someone else. So that might involve teasing, name-calling or making fun of them, making them feel scared or threatened, taking their things or damaging their property or spreading rumours about them. It could be posting something about them online – anything that intentionally makes them feel bad. That's the key thing that makes it different from banter: bullying is designed to cause hurt.

And why do people do it? Those who bully others often do so because they need to feel good about themselves or they need to feel some sort of power or control. It can be because something awful is going on in their lives and bullying is how they react. That's right, it's not just the target of the bullying who needs help – the bully may do too.

But that doesn't mean that we just let the bullying happen. Bullying is never OK, and if you are being bullied or see someone who is, it should always be reported to a responsible adult.

MYTH BUSTER

BOYS DON'T FIGHT

As we learned in chapter 1, throughout history boys have been assumed to be 'fighters'. Whether that's as the leader of the pack, as part of the military or just on a day-to-day basis. So when boys challenge each other, for example if someone is poking fun, often the first reaction is to physically fight. But this doesn't have to be the case – not all boys want to fight and neither should they need to. We are better than this! Fighting and violence are never necessary and don't solve anything. In fact, they often just make things worse. Fear, aggression and anger are strong emotions that we can use and learn from, but which don't have to result in violence. Simply taking a second, thinking about what you are feeling in the moment and why, then keeping your behaviour in check can lead to a much better result. It also means the next time someone pushes your buttons, you're less likely to get into fisticuffs. So in future, if you feel yourself heading for a brawl, why not deal with it by using your brain rather than your brawn?

Tips on beating bullying

If you are being bullied, please always remember that it can be stopped and you are never alone. There is always something that can be done about it or someone you can talk to. Don't ever feel like you have to deal with it by yourself.

HERE ARE SOME USEFUL POINTERS:

1) Your natural instinct may be to fight back immediately. Call it out by all means, but try not to retaliate physically. Act brave and walk away if you can. This is really hard to do and feels really unfair, but a reaction is exactly what the bullies want to see.

2) Tell a friend or adult (like a teacher, school nurse or counsellor, or parent/carer) about it straight away. They can take steps so that it stops and doesn't happen again. Even if they can't, it can help you feel less alone. If you feel like telling someone might make things worse, ask them to protect your identity and explain why. Just remember that if your safety is at risk, then certain people may have to be told to make sure you are not in any danger.

3) If you're struggling to speak up, keep a diary and show it to an adult to have a look at, or ask a friend to come with you when you speak to them.

4) Speak to a helpline like Childline or Bullying UK (you can search for them both online or find their details at the end of this book).

I know that all this involves a bit of bravery, but trust me – it's worth it to feel happy and safe in the long run.

On the other hand, if you see someone being bullied, step in if you feel it is safe to do so. It's important not to be a bystander. Still, I know that it isn't always possible or easy in the moment – in which case, check up on the person being bullied afterwards.

Are they OK? Do they need help? Do they need someone to go with them to speak to an adult about what is happening?

Perhaps they just need a friend and you could be that person. Simply knowing that someone is there in case they need to chat is hugely helpful.

BEATING BULLYING
CHARLIE CHRISTENSEN _ _ _ _ _ ■

Charlie is a twelve-year-old boy who was bullied for his love of musical theatre. He took his experience and launched the #cheerupcharlie online campaign in 2020, supported by numerous West End stars, which went viral. Charlie received a Diana Award for his efforts and is now an anti-bullying ambassador for the organisation. He tells us about stopping bullying and the advice he would give to any other young person going through the same thing.

Musical theatre allows me to get lost just for a while. Nothing matters apart from watching the performance or performing myself. I become part of the show almost.

At school my love of theatre was the main reason I was bullied so badly. People think that because it's theatre that makes me weird. I was called all sorts of horrid names and many times was kicked to the floor, where they took it in turns to kick or punch me. Mostly I'd curl up in a ball and wait for it to stop.

I used to try and ignore them, but no matter what people say, words hurt more than something physical. I'm making it my mission as a young changemaker to focus on acceptance. I encourage my generation to just be themselves and maybe then we'll create a generation of kids who are happy with just being themselves. Now when I get negative reactions, I turn it around and simply say, 'Yes, I do love it and always will – it's who I am.'

When people tell you to just ignore them, please don't hide away. If you get messages over social media, then share them. If it is to your face, then call them out. Talk to someone, even someone like me, who knows how you feel. I believe that talking is the answer. Don't suffer alone, because at the end of the day you are worth so much more than silence.

Everyone deserves to be who they are and follow their passions. For example, I'll never play football so don't tell me I should. We were made to be unique and that's what we need to encourage. Keep being unapologetically YOU!

MYTH BUSTER

BULLIES CAN'T CHANGE

If you've noticed some bullying behaviour in yourself, perhaps it's time to stop and ask yourself: How would I feel if that were me? Why am I doing this? What do I get out of making someone else unhappy? Is this something I need to talk to someone about? Do I have something in my life that is making me act this way and that I need help with? *Know this: there is no reason why you can't turn things around right now. You just have to be brave enough to admit that what you did was wrong and you're willing to change. Bullying doesn't automatically make you a bad person, but not admitting that it is wrong, and not wanting to change, does. Your first step is speaking to an adult about what's been going on, and when you're ready, perhaps apologising to the person who you may have affected. Trust me, everyone will feel better for it, including you.*

Gangs are not always good

As we explored earlier, being part of the gang can feel comforting, safe and like you have something you belong to. 'Boy gangs' can even be a positive thing if you can be yourself, be vulnerable, support each other when in need, and you respect those within and outside the group. If you can be true to yourself and not have to perform or put on a front, then they can really help you learn how to socialise, value others and build your own confidence. They can help you feel important, and that's great!

However, some gangs are not just people who like to hang out together. 'Gang' is also a word we use for groups of people who do things that are illegal or to hurt others. We see this especially in inner-city areas, and younger and younger people are getting involved in these activities – especially boys.

Unfortunately, a number of people have also got seriously hurt or even died because they've been involved in illegal gangs. I'm not trying to scare you just for the sake of it. As a doctor who works in Accident & Emergency, I've seen it first-hand. I've had to treat these young people and have seen the consequences.

Many of them have got into this situation without realising how bad it is and are struggling to get out. Often these people are punished if they try to leave the gang. If that's you or someone you know, get help straight away. Speak to an adult you can trust or speak to the police. Your safety matters more than anything else.

Being a good friend

Whether you are part of a group or you just have one or two close pals, being a good friend and having healthy friendships is something we should all try to do. Outside of our families, friends are people that are there for us not just to share good times and things we like with, but to help us out when things are tough. The best friendships involve recognising your own needs, the needs of those around you and how everyone can have their needs met. It also means not being scared to share your emotions, which can feel risky and make you feel vulnerable. Good friendships are those where all parties feel equal, seen and heard, and respected.

So often, boys are made to feel like they can't or shouldn't do this. We've all seen how the need to be 'masculine' can lead to a belief that you need to change yourself to fit in, be macho, perform and not show your feelings or emotions. That is exactly what this book is trying to change, and there's more on this in chapter 5.

So what does a positive friendship look like ?

Here are some qualities for you to think about:

Sharing our stuff,
if we all want to

Calling each
other out

Sticking up for
one another

Hanging out
together

Never needing
to perform

Saying sorry
when you
mess up

Talking to each
other about
difficult stuff

Welcoming
others

Celebrating the
good stuff

Respecting each
other's opinions

Supporting
each other

These are the sorts of things that I used to keep in mind when
I was growing up. And I found that I didn't just make friends
for school, I made friends for life.

Man in charge

People talk about how men should be good leaders, especially at work or in the family. It's something that you will need to think about as you grow up, because you might start feeling that expectation too, on the pitch, in school projects or even at home. But what does being a good leader involve?

Leadership is about so much more than just bossing people about – and as we've already seen, peer pressure can make people feel really uncomfortable. True leadership isn't about making someone do what you want – it's about being able to work in a team, recognising what others are good at and collectively doing better. It's also about trying to listen, understand and inspire those around you. So anyone can be a good leader if they want to – you'll notice that all these traits are things that women possess too – and they don't have to be bossy or act in a particular way. In fact, I think everyone should have a little bit of leadership in them, even if they're not the ones in charge.

LEARNING ABOUT LEADERSHIP
GETHIN JONES _ _ _ _ ■

Gethin Jones is a Welsh TV presenter and broadcaster. In 2022, Gethin got a degree in sport directorship, which is something he worked really hard for (and did really well at!). He's someone who knows what it takes to make a good leader and how we can all be one if we want. So here he tells us about the qualities and skills that we should all have.

Leadership is important because I can't think of a situation in my life where good leadership hasn't helped me improve, enhance and develop. So much can be achieved with the right person leading the way.

There are lots of different ways to lead, and being a good leader can be a really difficult task. Different personalities respond differently to others. I recently studied leadership in great detail. It's interesting how one style of leader can work in some situations, but be completely counterproductive in others. At the end of the day, you need to decide on what kind of leader YOU want to be, which is linked to who you are, your values and what is important to you.

So what makes a good leader? If you put 'leadership' into Google, you'll get over five billion hits. It's so incredibly subjective. Therefore, this is the toughest of questions, because different personalities will work differently to others and respond differently to a boss/leader/captain/coach. For example, person A might need reassurance and extra support, whilst person B may not want a fuss and just to be told directly what needs to be done. For me, trust is critical. Then honesty and flexibility (as I think this is a real sign of strength, ability and confidence). It takes a lot for a person in power (a leader) to say sorry. I see that as a super strength. A good leader doesn't need praise, is happy to be challenged, but isn't afraid of making the final decision.

As boys and men, we put pressure on ourselves to be 'manly', 'alpha' and 'confident'. But we sometimes don't realise that sensitivity, active listening or giving someone a hug can be all of those things! As a boy and younger brother, I was constantly trying to prove myself, to my classmates, teammates, family, sister . . . what a waste of energy! Enjoy the process of learning who you are first, then you can make decisions that can influence others in a positive way when you decide on a direction to go in life and in your career.

As for anyone who feels they aren't a natural-born leader, I hear this a lot. It's not about being a particular way. If you're inquisitive and you can listen, then when you choose what you're passionate about, you'll become the kind of leader YOU want to be.

This chapter has been about being mindful of our behaviour, especially towards others. So whether it's being a good captain on the field, feeling the pressure to be the 'man of the house' or simply being a good friend, hopefully these tips give you reassurance that there are loads of different ways to support and inspire others. People feel their best when they're being respected and having fun. I'm hoping that all the pointers from this chapter will set you well on your way to being a marvellous mate!

4

For as long as I can remember, I've battled with this body of mine. It's never felt quite right. I was too short as a kid. I always felt like I should lose weight so that my clothes fit better. I wanted to be muscly like the heroes in Marvel movies or all those ripped guys on Instagram. I wished my eyebrows weren't so darn big. That last one's actually not too bad right now because big brows are a thing, but they weren't when I was younger. I just wished I looked . . . well, perfect.

I still have thoughts like that sometimes. But rather than obsessing over them like I used to, I've learned to stop and remind myself: YOU ARE SO MUCH MORE THAN HOW YOU LOOK AND YOU DONT HAVE TO LOOK A CERTAIN WAY FOR ANYONE ELSE. What's more important is that you are healthy and happy with yourself. Just as being kind to others is important, being kind to yourself (and loving the way you are) is vital. Your body does so many amazing things, and its outward appearance is just one aspect.

If you're struggling with how you look right now, I totally get how you feel. It's really common to worry about that sort of thing as you're growing up. But I'm hoping I can teach you how (and why) to be friends with your body and appreciate it for all the wonderful things it does. Let's start with the hard work it's doing right now as you grow from a boy into a man.

Pubes, penises and smelly pits . . .

Your body is incredible. It does so many different things every day, many of them without you even realising. From your eyes being able to differentiate between millions of colours, to the electrical impulses travelling around your nervous system at over 400 kilometres per hour, to the cells of your skin replacing themselves every month, it's all pretty spectacular. But I want to concentrate on one particular bit of awesomeness: puberty.

Just a note before I dive in: this book isn't a puberty guide. It's only going to touch on certain parts of it. But if you do want a bit more detail (and loads of other great stuff) you can always check out my book *HOW TO GROW UP (AND FEEL AMAZING!)*. OK, let's crack on. Puberty is the process that your body goes through when you are growing from a child into an adult. You may or may not have reached this stage of life already. In actual fact, people start puberty at different ages (usually anywhere from nine to fourteen years old), and it has nothing to do with how 'masculine' you are.

So don't freak out if your body hasn't started changing yet. I was a late bloomer too, and *boy* did it stress me out. For a long time I was the shortest kid in class and I didn't start puberty until after my friends, so I really looked like the odd one out. But I can assure you that it'll happen in time and you'll realise that there's no need to worry. If it is playing on your mind, then a chat with your doctor or nurse might help calm your fears.

Puberty gets going when your body starts to produce lots of hormones. These are chemicals that are made in specific parts of the body that then go on to make changes all around it. During puberty, everything is rapidly growing and changing in preparation for you to become a man.

It's not just your body that changes. Your brain is also going through puberty, and that affects the way you think and feel about everything. It's not unusual for your feelings to be all over the place right now. Don't worry, because that will settle. We'll talk a bit more about feelings, especially in relation to your mental health, in the next chapter.

Your bits, your business

One area in which you will definitely experience change is your 'boy parts' (or to use the technical term: penis and testicles, a.k.a. genitals). During puberty these will grow, change colour and shape, and get hairier. Everyone's will change at a different rate and they'll all look different too.

For some reason, some boys and men LOVE to obsess over the size of their bits and compare themselves to others. Some will even claim that a bigger penis somehow makes you more of a man or more masculine (yep, it's that word again). Those horrible 'locker-room moments' are something that many of us will be familiar with, growing up. This is utter rubbish. Genitals come in all shapes and sizes and their appearance has no impact whatsoever on who you are or what you are capable of.

DON'T
BELIEVE
ME?

Then consider this: our opinions about penis size have changed throughout history. For example, the ancient Greeks used to think that smaller penises were more beautiful, and larger ones were ugly. That's why all those ancient Greek statues have smaller penises!

The way your genitals look is determined by so much that is out of your control: where you are from in the world, your genetic make-up and possibly even what happens to you before you are born. You should feel confident that no matter how you look, you are just the way you are supposed to be. Try not to let other people's opinions affect you. I know this is difficult because we live in a world obsessed with appearance. But what is in your pants is no one else's business – unless you choose for it to be!

If it's something that is worrying you, remember that right now your body is still changing and things will probably look quite different once you have finished growing. I'll let you into a little secret that no one ever tells you: most people worry about their bits growing up, but we turn out absolutely fine in the end. Again, if you are really concerned, have a chat with your doctor.

Less hair? More hair? Don't care!

Getting more hair is part of the puberty journey. And it's another thing that people might use as a measure of masculinity. And – you guessed it –

this is nonsense too!

The amount of hair you have on your face or body has nothing to do with how 'manly' you are. Like other aspects of your appearance, it's all down to a number of different factors (like your family history and genetics).

I really struggled to grow a proper beard when I was younger. I couldn't do it properly until my early twenties. It was even later for some of my friends. And with the benefit of hindsight, I can tell you this: whether we had facial hair or not didn't matter at all.

Different people and cultures see facial and body hair differently. In some traditions and religions, it's important to keep your hair. For example, in Sikhism, which is the religion of my family, not cutting your hair is seen as a sacred thing. Others like to keep certain hair trimmed or short, such as in Islamic traditions. You might have seen on social media that many men will trim or even shave off their body hair completely. Basically, it's as much about personal preference as it is anything else.

If you like to keep your hair, then go for it. If not, then that's absolutely your choice too. Whether you choose to keep a beard and trim your pubes, or the other way round, it's totally up to you. You do you!

Is image everything?

Puberty can really play on your mind and affect the way you think about yourself and your body. I want you to love your body for what it does, not just the way it looks. The way you see yourself and think about your body is something we call **BODY IMAGE** and it's about time we talked more about this because it's a huge thing for boys.

When we look in the mirror, we can be negative and critical about ourselves: *I don't like that part or I want to change that bit of my body.* This isn't always good or helpful, and can make us forget what's great about ourselves.

A few years ago I did a photoshoot for a daytime TV show called *Loose Women*. It was me and a bunch of famous men all in our underwear. Yes, it was exactly as nerve-racking as it sounds! I was terrified because taking my clothes off in front of strangers isn't something I do that often. The shoot was to show that we all come in different shapes, colours and sizes, and we all have hang-ups about ourselves no matter who we are or what we look like.

As fun as it was, there was a really important message behind this campaign: to get men and boys talking about their bodies. For so long, people have believed that only girls worry about their body image. The truth is that boys share the same worries too, and having a positive, healthy body image is as important for them as anyone else, which is what we're going to explore next.

BE GOOD TO YOURSELF
GOK WAN _____ ■

Gok Wan is one of the most talented people I know: he cooks, is a stylist and fashion expert, and is a super-successful DJ! Gok has also spoken about his battles with his body as he struggled with growing up overweight. Here he talks about why it's important to love your body and how the way you look doesn't determine who you are, or what your worth is.

When I was growing up, I probably had more hang-ups than a cloakroom! But they didn't really kick in until my early teens. I guess prior to that, because I'd spent so much time at home with my family and in my family business, life was very simple because we were surrounded by love, customers, food and acceptance.

It wasn't until my early teens that I started to find my social independence and realised that I looked different to everybody else – particularly in terms of my size. I was an overweight child, and even though I didn't have much of a problem with it (because I was used to it), it wasn't until people made comments about my weight and called me names that I developed those hang-ups. On top of that I had acne and greasy hair and just felt very unattractive.

Having gone through all that and been various different shapes and sizes since, I've learned that rather than worrying what other people think of you,

it's important to love, respect and look after yourself and do what is best for

YOU.

If you want to be truly happy and make the most of life, remember that your worth is not determined by how you look, but by who you are and what your actions are. You are so much more than your physical appearance. Be you, have ambition, work hard, be a good person, try to look after your health and remember your body is precious – nothing else matters!

Exercise for health, not for likes

One way of keeping your body happy is by exercising. Being physically active builds muscle strength, makes your bones stronger, keeps your joints mobile, makes your heart and cardiovascular system fitter, and is really good for your mental health. The more active you are, the more you will be able to do and the better you will feel. You can get the physical activity you need at school and all the other hobbies you might be involved in. But, like anything, it is possible to take it too far.

Some boys (especially in their teens) like to go to the gym because they want to build muscle and look a certain way. They might also think that being buff makes you more of a man. Newsflash: it doesn't! You'll probably have seen images of muscled-up guys on social media: massive arms and abs for days. That might be great for them, but it can make people who follow them feel like they have to look that way too. Seeing lots of images like these isn't great for your self-esteem either.

When you see these sorts of images, please remember that not everyone is meant to look the same. Much of how we are is determined by our genetics, which is totally out of our control. I made my peace with the fact that I'm not going to be a 6-foot-tall basketball player a long time ago! There are also tons of super-successful athletes and models with a huge variety of body shapes. Have a think about people who have done amazing things in the world and ask yourself: **HOW MUCH DOES WHAT THEY LOOK LIKE CONTRIBUTE TO WHAT THEY'VE ACHIEVED AND DOES IT REALLY MATTER TO ME?** Chances are they are amazing because of so much more than just their muscle mass!

Many of these pictures of muscly men will also have been enhanced or altered to make them look better. Also, I'll let you in on a secret: I know as a doctor that super-ripped people have to work out for hours and hours every day, are only allowed to eat certain things to get enough protein in (like endless portions of boiled chicken) and may even have personal chefs and trainers to help. It's a full-time job to look that way.

Here's my opinion: there is no point having a six-pack if you're miserable because you can't enjoy your life. Don't get me wrong, if you have a six-pack and you're perfectly happy with your life then great! I just don't think people should be punishing themselves with gruelling diets and workouts to look like a DC comic character or someone on social media (who's probably not real anyway!).

I always tell my young patients that you should try to exercise for your health, not your looks. If you've been advised to manage your weight by a medical professional, then exercise may also be a part of this. However, for everyone else it should be a normal part of life and, above all, it should be fun! You can exercise through sports, games, walking, cycling, gymnastics, whatever you fancy. For me it's dancing!

BEING AT THE TOP OF YOUR GAME
MICHAEL GUNNING _ _ _ _ ▪

Michael Gunning is a Jamaican–British competitive swimmer who has competed in the World Aquatics Championships and is a Jamaican national record holder in various events. He is a proud advocate for LGBTQ+ people in sport and has spoken out about racism in swimming. He is also one of the kindest people I have ever met! Here he tells us about his love of sport and how anyone can learn to take part.

I had bundles of energy when I was younger, and it was great to put that energy into many different sports. I tried everything: football, tennis and rugby, but the sport I loved most was swimming, and I wanted to challenge myself to see how fast I could be in the water.

It's an incredible feeling competing on an international level because everyone has worked so hard to get there. I felt extremely nervous representing my country, but I remembered why I started swimming in the first place and just enjoyed the competitions and racing against the best athletes in the world.

Dedication, determination, hard work and effective time-management were all really important to get me there. Swimming has really helped me in so many ways because all the skills I learnt while training and competing taught me discipline, which fed down into my studies and other areas of my life.

That's why I think more people should try to get into sport! Despite not being good at every sport I tried, it's great setting goals and challenges, as you'll uncover some of your greatest strengths and skills. Sport has a wonderful way of uniting people around the world no matter who you are, and some of my greatest friends are athletes I used to race against.

Food for fuel (and fun) . . .

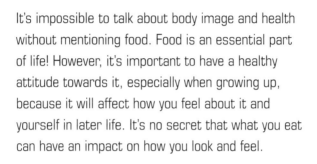

It's impossible to talk about body image and health without mentioning food. Food is an essential part of life! However, it's important to have a healthy attitude towards it, especially when growing up, because it will affect how you feel about it and yourself in later life. It's no secret that what you eat can have an impact on how you look and feel.

When you see all those 'perfect bodies' in the media, what you don't see are the strict dietary regimes that people put themselves through to achieve that look. These can be really restrictive and even unhealthy if you don't know what you're doing. Unfortunately that doesn't stop people trying to achieve the same results.

Sadly these sorts of images can lead to the development of eating disorders, which affect boys as well as girls. Boys may not realise it's happening because they become so focused on obtaining that 'perfect' physique and think that this is the only way to do it. Those who do recognise a problem may not feel like they can speak up because they might feel embarrassed about their feelings or think it's not a very 'masculine' thing to do. All of this means that we probably don't see the true extent of the issue.

CLUES THAT ALTERED EATING BEHAVIOUR COULD BE TURNING INTO A DISORDER INCLUDE:

Constantly worrying about what or how much you've eaten

Making yourself sick after eating

Deliberately restricting the amount of food you eat

Being secretive about what you eat

We can all have some of these thoughts and behaviours occasionally, but they are usually temporary. However, if you've noticed them quite a lot then it's really important that you speak to someone about it. If you can't speak to someone you know, there are helplines at the end of this book.

Remember that food is there to fuel your body and brain. We need it to stay healthy and to provide us with the energy to grow and do the things we need to do. Sure, we all have to be sensible, which is why you'll hear healthcare professionals always talking about having a balanced diet and eating things in moderation (especially things that have lots of sugar or fat). However, the underlying message should always be the same: food is essential and is there to be enjoyed.

Having a healthy and positive body image is part of looking after and loving yourself. What you eat and do will have an impact, but at the end of the day, it's much more about how you think. So I want you to say to yourself: **NO MATTER HOW I LOOK, I'M GOING TO LOOK AFTER ME!**

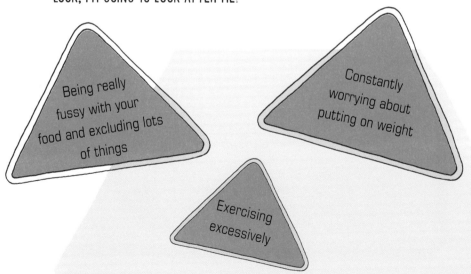

Being really fussy with your food and excluding lots of things

Constantly worrying about putting on weight

Exercising excessively

MAN OF THE MOMENT: FREDDIE FLINTOFF

Freddie Flintoff is a TV presenter and cricketing legend. In 2005 he won the BBC Sports Personality of the Year award and in 2006 he was given an MBE by the Queen for his achievements. What most people may not realise is that Freddie also suffered from an eating disorder during his cricket career – something that he kept secret. His disorder came from a worry about putting on too much weight (apparently people used to call him the 'fat cricketer'). It got so bad that he used to make himself sick after eating meals (something we call bulimia). Fortunately, he eventually overcame his disorder, but it took a long time for him to ask for help. Things could have turned out very differently if he hadn't, which is why it's so important to speak up if you're going through a hard time like this. Eating disorders, like any other illness, can affect anyone and you should never be ashamed or embarrassed to speak up.

I hope that at the end of this section, you're thinking about yourself in a much more positive light – and recognising how amazing you already are! I'm going to finish this chapter with something a bit different. I want you to go and listen to some music that makes you feel good about yourself. You can even have a little dance if you like! If you need a suggestion, check out 'Good as Hell' by Lizzo (one of my faves!). It's all about loving yourself no matter who you are or what you look like. It always makes me feel great!

BREAKING

DOWN

BARRIERS

5

Let's move on from talking about your body . . .
and now concentrate on your brain. What's that got
to do with being a boy, you ask? Well, if you're
going to be the best version of yourself,
you also need to understand your feelings.

I know what you might be thinking: **URGH, I DONT LIKE TALKING ABOUT THAT STUFF!** If that's you, it's quite understandable. This is an area that boys (and men) aren't always good at talking about and they don't always get permission to. They don't get taught how, and society has traditionally expected them to be strong, in control and in charge. (Remember those words we associated with masculinity in chapter 1?)

The reality is that sometimes we feel like everything is sorted and under control, and at other times we feel not so great. Either way, boys and men need to get better at showing, talking about and dealing with whatever we are experiencing, especially the more negative stuff. And that means breaking down some of the barriers that might be stopping us from sharing. So let's get into it . . .

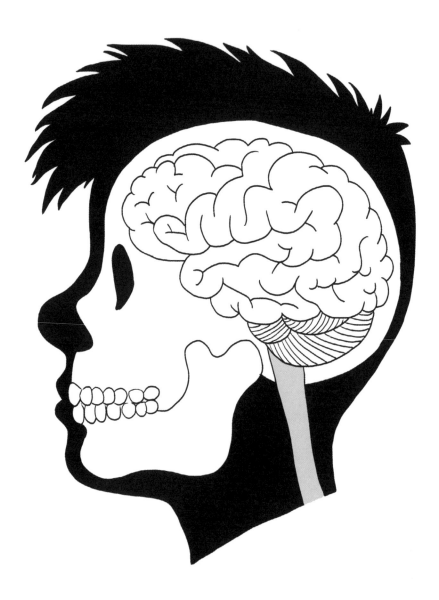

Mental health is key

Mental health is the term we use to describe how we feel and how we deal with the challenges of everyday life. It's something we all have. Mental health and wellbeing are HUGE topics of conversation right now. You will have heard about them on TV or online and you may have talked about them at school. Some of us will have personal experiences of mental health problems, either ourselves or with people we know.

Just as it's important to look after your body, it's crucial to look after your mind as well so that it can work at its best too. We can do this in lots of ways: through being mindful of what we put into our bodies (our diet and nutrition) or what we do with them (through physical activity and sleep). We can also do it through being better at expressing and managing our feelings and emotions. That's a little trickier than eating healthily or getting more exercise, but I'm going to show you how being more aware of your emotions not only makes your mind work better, but makes you a better person too.

Riding the emotional rollercoaster

It's easy for me to say that boys and men should be able to express their emotions more, but it isn't always simple or straightforward. You're probably going through a time in life when it feels like your emotions are all over the place. Some days you're calm and enjoying life, and on others it feels like you're about to fly off the handle in a rage at the slightest inconvenience. It's like you're on an emotional rollercoaster!

Don't worry, this can be completely normal for two main reasons . . .

When you're growing up and your brain is still maturing, you rely more on parts of the brain that deal with emotions and feelings to make decisions, rather than the logical thinking bits. Using your emotions (like love, lust, pain, fear or anger) to make your decisions means that you're less likely to think them through rationally. So it's no surprise that you might not always make the best decisions in the moment!

At the same time, your body is making lots of hormones (remember the puberty stuff?) which are all flying around and also having an effect on how you feel. Put it all together, and

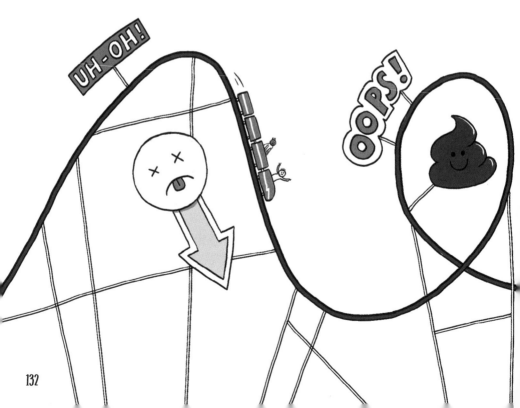

it's the perfect melting pot! This is precisely why some boys act out during this time of life, while others struggle with their feelings and may even go through a really difficult time with their mental health.

At this point, you're probably thinking that emotions sound like a bit of a hassle. It's true that some can be hard to deal with, but at the same time, the tough ones can help teach us lessons and allow us to grow as people. When we feel and process difficult emotions, we learn how to manage them better next time. In that way, we turn them into something useful. Also, sometimes the hard feelings are our brain's way of telling us that something might be wrong (so we can sort out the cause), and that we might need to ask for help.

The feeling spectrum

Feelings can broadly be grouped into 'positive' ones (like love, happiness, kindness) and 'negative' ones (like fear, hate, anger). What I've noticed is that boys are more likely to internalise the positive ones (so they're less likely to openly show love and compassion for their peers because it's perceived as less masculine) and externalise the negative ones (like lashing out when someone annoys you or doing something drastic like punching a wall). All boys (and men) would be better off knowing that it's OK to externalise the positive ones more, and we should be better at expressing and managing the negative ones. That includes speaking up when you are feeling sad, hurt or down. This isn't an admission of defeat or anything bad on your part, but a very responsible way of dealing with something that feels hard.

Growing up, I hated dealing with difficult emotions. When I went through anything tricky I actively avoided the unpleasant feelings and never spoke about them. I just put them in a sort of 'mental box'. I would never speak up when I was sad, because I didn't think that anyone would understand or be able to help. I actually became really good at hiding it and not processing it at all.

Then, as an adult, I ended up having counselling because there were times when I really struggled with my emotions (especially showing them). I realised that all those things I had done as a child weren't helpful any more! That took a long time for me to work out and I had a lot of barriers in my mind to break down. Lots of boys and men have similar experiences. They too might struggle to express and cope with their emotions and they might not ask for help when they need to. They might also develop bad habits and unhealthy behaviours to cope. All of this can have a negative impact on them and the people they know.

So I'm telling you this now: feeling and talking about your emotions (especially when you're struggling or going through a tough time) is normal. Emotions are OK! Emotions are what makes us human! Being what we call 'emotionally intelligent' means that you'll be more sensitive to your own needs and those of others. It will help you understand yourself and those around you better. And all of that makes you a better person. Never be scared to say or express how you feel. And if you're finding it hard to cope, reach out and speak to someone. You matter. Your feelings matter. And you can feel better!

MYTH BUSTER

BOYS CRY TOO

It's important to understand the difference between managing our emotions and ignoring them or bottling them up. Forcing yourself to suppress your emotions is never good. This goes for crying too. Many of us will have heard the saying 'big boys don't cry' or phrases like 'man up'. This is some of the worst advice anyone could give you. It's important for boys and men to be able to express true emotions if they need to. Otherwise it could lead to even bigger problems later. Sometimes having a cry just for you when you're feeling a certain way can really help you feel so much better. Think of it as an emotional pressure-release valve that pops off every now and again! If you're someone who feels like they cry easily, that's not a bad thing either. Some of us are much more emotionally connected with ourselves than others. Also, don't be afraid to do it in front of others if you have to. And if someone does it in front of you and you feel a bit uncomfortable, remember that these are natural feelings. You don't always have to fix the situation. Just being there and being supportive might be enough!

THE IMPORTANCE OF FEELINGS

ALEXIS CAUGHT_ _ _ _ ▪

Alexis Caught is an amazing author, crisis counsellor, psychotherapist, model and rugby player. He's someone who is really passionate about mental health and speaking up when you are struggling. Here he tells us about the importance of expressing your emotions and the importance of being kind to yourself.

Masculinity and feelings have ALWAYS gone together. The problem is, society at large has just said we're only 'allowed' to feel certain feelings (like anger or pride), which unfortunately aren't very good for us. Anger in particular is a masking emotion . . . we tend to use it when we're trying to hide other difficult feelings we're not 'supposed' to feel, like fear, sadness, loneliness and worry. So we cover these up and express them through anger.

When we mask our emotions, push them down and deny them, they don't actually go away. They build up and toxify, often becoming dangerous. If we can be honest about how we feel (rather than masking our vulnerability with anger) then we're more likely to get the help and support that we need and deserve.

As a therapist, a large part of my work is helping people really check in, connect with and understand how they're feeling. We may quickly leap for words like anger or frustrated to describe how we feel, but take a moment, steady your breathing, close your eyes and pay attention to how your body feels. Give yourself time to be honest with yourself about how you really feel. What's making you feel like that, and what do you need to feel better? Getting to know ourselves and connect with our emotions, in a world which discourages boys and men from being self-reflective, is an act of courage and defiance.

So when I'm having a tough day, the first thing I do is immediately re-assess my 'to do' list. If something happened or I felt bad, I used to try and struggle on regardless. Over time, I learned that helps no one. Now, I feel confident to let go of some of the pressure, take some of the weight off and lighten my load when the world and my feelings just seem heavier sometimes. Allowing myself to rest is an act of self-love, which ultimately means I have fewer bad days because I deal with things (my feelings) at the start, without letting them grow bigger and more challenging.

For anyone struggling to express themselves or be who they really are, know that you're not alone. So many people are struggling to understand and express themselves; it's confusing, it can be scary – but it's worth it. Secondly, imagine if there were no nay-saying parents/teachers/money/bills. What would your life look like and how can you most make it reflect that? Finally, on days when you're struggling and feeling alone, just know that there is a team of friendly people at SHOUT 85258, a free, confidential text line, open 24/7, 365 days a year, who are here to listen to you and support you.

Mental health problems

OK, so what happens when those normal day-to-day difficult feelings get out of control and you can't cope? What happens if the tough ones don't seem to go away? What if they start to stop you from doing the things you need to do? This is when you need to think about whether they are turning into mental health PROBLEMS – something that boys and men aren't great at opening up about. Understanding this helps you to not only recognise when you might need help to get back on track, but also look out for your friends and family too.

Clues that what you're going through might be a mental health issue include:

- Feeling sad or down most of the time and not being able to enjoy the things you normally would

- Feeling a lot of worry or guilt, which is stopping you from doing things

- Not being able to sleep properly

- Having a lack of motivation to do anything at all

- Isolating yourself from other people

- Feeling bad about eating, not eating normally, or eating and then making yourself sick

- Feeling the need to do things over and over again to feel safe or calm

- Feeling like you want to hurt yourself or someone else

There are lots of different kinds of mental health problem. You may even have heard of some of them, such as anxiety, depression and self-harm:

ANXIETY

Feeling anxious is completely normal. For instance, if you have an exam or audition coming up. It's part of the natural fight-or-flight response we have to keep us safe if we think we are in danger. Usually these feelings of anxiety settle down, but they become an issue if they happen for no reason, if they are severe and we can't control them, or if they don't go away.

DEPRESSION

Depression is the medical term we use to describe feelings of low mood or sadness for long periods of time. Again, it's normal to feel down now and again, but people with depression can't shake the feeling off and it affects their ability to do the things they normally would.

SELF-HARM

Self-harm is where someone is struggling with their feelings and emotions so much that they need to hurt themselves to cope. They're not doing it through choice or attention-seeking, but because they can't cope with how they're feeling any other way. Often they will also hide any signs of it so that others don't find out.

There are other kinds of mental health issue too, such as the eating disorders we discussed in the last chapter. If you recognise any of these in yourself, it's really important to speak to an adult, medical professional or helpline (see the resources section at the end of this book). It could just be that you need a bit of reassurance. Or it could be that you need more professional help, such as counselling or medication. However, you won't know for sure or get the help you need unless you speak up.

Often, boys and men don't feel like they can open up and talk about what they're going through. This means that they don't get the support they need and things can get worse. In the worst cases, people have taken their own lives because they feel like there is no other way out. This is a really difficult subject to talk about.

Why? Research shows that when boys and young men feel like they have to conform to certain kinds of masculinity, it has a negative impact on their mental health and increases their risk of wanting to harm themselves. This has to change. It's precisely the reason I'm writing this book. I want all boys and young men to know that it's OK to be exactly who you are. You don't have to act a certain way. Being yourself not only keeps you happy, but it also means you're less likely to hurt yourself. You deserve to be you and you deserve to be here!

If you've been having thoughts about hurting yourself, then I want you to speak to someone straight away, at home, school

THERE IS ALWAYS SOMEONE OUT THERE WILLING TO HELP.

or a helpline. As someone who felt just like this at times when I was growing up, I am proof that it doesn't have to be like this and you can feel better. And no matter how you feel, you are NEVER alone.

YOU CAN FEEL BETTER

JONNY BENJAMIN _ _ _ _ ■

Jonny Benjamin is an award-winning mental health campaigner, film producer, speaker and writer. Jonny's viewpoint on mental health is so important because not only has he had his own mental health difficulties, but he understands how mental health and being a boy relate to each other. Here he tells us how his experiences with his mental health have shaped who he is and why speaking up is the first step to feeling better.

My mental health was a challenge growing up. My parents first took me to a child psychologist at the age of five. However, it was never properly discussed, especially when I was at a school. My primary school was an all-boys school and I always felt totally different compared to all the other boys. I wish someone would have just told me that I wasn't 'weird' or 'crazy'. However, now I go into schools myself and give talks on my experiences to help young people, especially boys, realise they're not alone. So I feel that something good has ultimately come out of my struggles when I was growing up.

I wish other people knew the difference their actions make when someone is going through a mental health challenge. For me personally, just a simple message to check in can make all the difference. The worst thing that people around me can do is avoid the subject. It creates an awkwardness that doesn't help anyone. I know it can still be embarrassing to talk about mental health but we need to get over that shame. We would never shy away from a physical health issue like diabetes. We have to start addressing mental health much more equally to physical health than we currently do.

I still think there's an issue with men and mental health. For many, struggling with mental health, and asking for help, is a huge weakness. I find that 'self-care' is seen as something quite feminine. It shouldn't be that way. Boys and men generally tend to focus more on their physical fitness, but we need to be encouraging them to look after their mental fitness in the same way. I think we'll get there. It often takes time for traditional ways of thinking and behaving to change.

A young person struggling with their mental health should never feel ashamed or embarrassed if they're having difficult thoughts and feelings. It's unbelievably common. Secondly, finding an outlet for those thoughts and feelings can be so helpful. I used to keep a diary when I was growing up. I also found poetry and songwriting useful. Ultimately, this eventually gave me the confidence to ask for help, which was the key to change for my mental wellbeing. There are a range of excellent sources of support out there for young people now, from Shout to The Mix, so please do make good use of them! Reaching out to organisations for assistance when I needed to was a lifeline for me during my darkest times growing up.

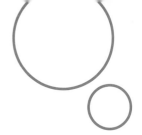

Tips for better mental wellbeing

Over the years, I've learned that there are lots of things we can all do to keep our mental health in good shape. I've used some of them myself and you might find them useful too:

1) Speak up – first and foremost, being honest and open about difficult thoughts and feelings is the first (and most brave) step to getting help. Always talk to a trusted adult when you are struggling.

2) Write it down – a diary or a worry box can be a great way of getting your feelings out, and you can go through them with an adult.

3) Look after your body and mind – physical activity, eating healthy food and paying attention to getting good-quality sleep are all really good for our mental wellbeing.

4) Practise mindfulness – you may have learned about this in school already or you can find mindfulness exercises online.

5) Be careful online – the internet and social media can be really useful and fun, but they can potentially be harmful too. If being online is making you feel bad, remember it's not the real world and you can always step away and speak to someone.

Turn your mindset into a 'kindset'

The biggest tip I can give you about looking after your own mental wellbeing, and that of those around you, is to be kind. It sounds really corny, but there is good science showing that when we are kind it has a really positive effect on our brains. It's such a simple thing, but it makes a huge difference and anyone can do it.

Don't be afraid to be kind to others, especially if they might be going through something you don't know or understand. We can all do with a kind friend sometimes. And don't forget about yourself. You're allowed to be kind to yourself when things are tough. Remind yourself that it's OK not to feel OK and there is always someone there to support you during hard times.

And you can apply this principle to your whole life! When you try to think and do everything from a place of kindness, this is what I call a 'kindset'. Not only does it help you feel great about yourself, but it will make things better for those around you too. Try it today and see what happens. I promise you won't be disappointed!

THE COMPLETE

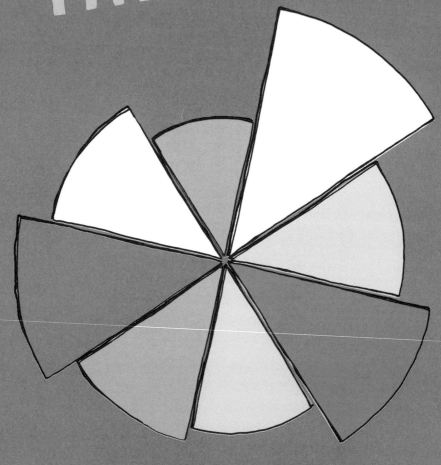

YOU

?

Do you remember back in chapter 1, I asked you some questions about words you associate with being a boy or man? Here's a reminder:

Leader	Artistic	Focused	Brave	Musical
Assertive	Creative	Camp	Beautiful	
Caring	Protective	Ambitious	Rugged	
Gentle	Tender	Strong	Intelligent	
	Kind			
Professional	Funny	Macho		
				Laddish
Emotional	Understanding	Ally		

Grab that piece of paper where you wrote down the words you think best describe boys and men. Now that you've read the book (well done for sticking with it!), do you think you would change any of your answers? Go through the list from the last page again and see if there are more words you would include. Are there any words you would use that aren't on the list?

What you should now understand is that boys and men can have lots of different, and equally amazing, qualities. There is no one way you have to be. If masculinity is just a word to describe men and boys, then it is so much more than what you might have thought before – in fact, when we think about words that describe POSITIVE masculinity, there are no real wrong answers, only different ones for different people.

THAT MEANS YOU ARE FREE TO BE WHOEVER AND HOWEVER YOU WANT TO BE

Be kind

No matter who or how you choose to be, one thing I do want you to remember is to be kind. If you've been paying attention, you'll have noticed that much of this book asks you to think about and show kindness. Why is that? Because kindness to both yourself and others is one simple way of being better than before. And it's something we can all do.

Showing kindness, compassion and respect to others makes the world a better place. Plus, it won't just make you a better person – positive people attract positive vibes. And remember: your vibe attracts your tribe! So you may well find yourself surrounded by a few more friends too.

Being kind to yourself means acknowledging the great things about you and valuing them. It also means not being too hard on yourself if things aren't how you want them to be. No one is perfect, we all make mistakes and some things are just out of our control. So show yourself a bit of self-care and self-love now and again! Give yourself time to learn and grow – you'll soon get the hang of it.

BEING THE BEST YOU
JORDAN WYLIE _____ ◼

Jordan is an inspirational author, extreme adventurer and charity fundraiser. He's a former soldier who is now the UK's ambassador for the Army Cadet Force, and he is a motivational speaker for young people in schools and colleges. Here's his advice on being your best self.

We are all capable of doing great things in this world when we find the best version of ourselves, but before we can do that, we have to be prepared to step out of our comfort zone in order to stretch, grow and develop into that special person, which will allow us to achieve our full potential in all areas of our lives. Always be grateful for the positive aspects of your life such as loved ones, family, friends, opportunities and experiences. An attitude of gratitude will take you a long way and open new doors on the journey to become the best version of you.

I think it's important to understand that being brave doesn't mean you aren't scared, nervous or apprehensive about a situation. Bravery isn't something you are born with, either, but it is something you can develop and practise as you face challenges and overcome adversity in life. I have found that taking responsibility for my actions (including my mistakes) and facing my fears head on is the best way to develop bravery. I also try to focus on the things I can control and not worry about the things that I can't. Of course, this can be easier said than done sometimes. One of the best pieces of advice I was ever given as a soldier, which I use these days as an extreme adventurer, is to 'get comfortable with being uncomfortable'!

Life growing into a young man can be very hectic, stressful and daunting sometimes. There are so many changes going on in our bodies during this period. It is really important that we 'check in' with ourselves on a regular basis. I try to be aware of my thoughts and feelings daily to ensure my mental and physical wellbeing is on track. I find regular exercise, sharing my problems with others and having personal short- and long-term goals also helps me stay focused and moving in the right direction at all times.

I think the easiest and most effective way to build kindness into our everyday life is to simply practise it daily! We can do this very easily by helping those around us where we can, supporting those less fortunate and trying to always consider the impact of our words and actions on other people. Act with empathy at all times – this means putting yourself in someone else's shoes and seeing things from their perspective. Other ways to practise kindness are through active listening to others, never forgetting your manners and respecting everyone regardless of their differences. Kindness is infectious and the world needs much more of it!

As a former frontline combat soldier, people often had pre-conceived ideas about how I should live my life and the things I should do. I would never have considered telling one of my superiors that I wasn't feeling well and I was struggling mentally due to being judged or seen as a weaker member of the team. These days, though, I talk openly and confidently about my feelings, my emotions and the challenges I face without feeling embarrassed at all in any way. Positive masculinity to me is about being yourself without fearing how you will be judged by others.

Where do we go now?

This is the bit where I hand over to you. If you weren't sure about what it really takes to be an amazing boy and man, I hope everything you have read has reassured you and made you believe that you've got this. You were already brilliant, but I'm hoping that you now feel inspired to go on and be even better.

Now it's time to take everything you've learned and put it into action. So here's your final task: go out and be the best you can be. I know you can and you will.

IT'S TIME TO SHOW THE WORLD YOUR COMPLETE, TRUEST AND MOST AWESOME SELF.

Resources

Here are some useful sites that you can go to for more
information about the things discussed in this book:

Bullying
- **Family Lives** bullying.co.uk
- **Anti-Bullying Alliance** anti-bullyingalliance.org.uk

Mental health and wellbeing
- **YoungMinds** youngminds.org.uk
- **Beat** beateatingdisorders.co.uk
- **Papyrus** papyrus-uk.org

Sex and sexuality
- **BISH** bishuk.com

General life advice
- **The Mix** themix.org.uk

Here are some helplines in case you need to speak to someone
confidentially:

Childline childline.org.uk – 0800 1111
Switchboard LGBT+ Helpline switchboard.lgbt – 0300 330 0630
Shout giveusashout.org – text 'SHOUT' to 85258

Index

allies 39–43, 46, 56, 58, 61,
   62, 65, 66–7, 73, 74–5,
   78–9
allyship 37, 43, 46, 58, 62,
   66–7,74–5, 78
ancient Greece 16, 111
ancient India 18–20, 25
ancient Rome 17
asexual 30

Benjamin, Jonny 144–5
biological sex 15, 24–5, 30
biphobia 35, 41
bisexual 30, 32, 35
Black Lives Matter 68–9, 72
body image 114–20, 123–5
bullying 41, 44–6, 62, 64, 68,
   85, 89, 91–4, 95–6, 97

Caught, Alexis 137–9
characteristics 11–17, 19–20,
   24, 28, 31, 33, 150
Christensen, Charlie 95–6
cisgender 25
confidence 9, 27, 31, 33, 98,
   104, 105, 111, 138, 145
consent 49–52, 88
Cox, Laverne 57
culture 15, 18–21, 23–5, 28,
   32–3, 48, 62, 69, 72, 113

eating disorders 123–6, 140,
   142
Eddo-Lodge, Reni 71
Einstein, Albert 4
Elba, Idris 21
emotions 8, 16–17, 22, 23, 28,
   66, 92, 99–100, 131–41,
   153, 154
equality 22, 48, 56, 58–61, 67,
   78, 99
exercise 118–20, 131, 146,
   153

Farah, Mo 21
femininity 24, 34
feminism 56–9, 61
Flintoff, Freddie 126
food 123–6, 131, 140, 146
friendship 39, 63, 73, 82–5,
   93–4, 99–101, 105, 147,
   151, 152

gender 15, 18–21, 23–5, 28,
   30–33, 42, 53, 55, 58, 66,
   75, 77
gender fluid 25
gender identity 24–5, 33
gender non-binary 25
gender stereotypes 20–21, 35,
   42, 53
genetics 15, 111–12, 119

Graf, Jake 26–8, 42
Gunning, Michael 121–2

heterosexual 30–31, 35, 62
homophobia 35, 41, 46, 90
homosexual 30

indigenous Americans 20, 25

Jeung, Russell 71
Jones, Gethin 103–4

Kaepernick, Colin 70
kindness 7, 9, 28, 33, 36, 54,
    77, 107, 121, 134, 147,
    150–51, 153–4
King, Martin Luther 70

Lanji, Ryan 32–3
leadership 16–17, 20, 22, 42,
    61, 70, 92, 102–5
LGBTQ+ 30, 35–6, 41, 45,
    62–7, 74, 89, 90, 121

Marshall, Yanis 21
masculinity 7– 9, 11–15, 18–21,
    23–5, 28–31, 34, 37, 100,
    109–12, 123, 129, 134,
    137, 142, 144, 150, 154
  history of 14–18
  toxic 7, 9, 23
mental health 62, 109, 118,
    129–47, 153, 154
misogyny 55–6, 74

Morris, Emma 60–61
Mukherjee, Sabyasachi 21

Neanderthals 14–15, 21

Obama, Barack 22
Ocasio-Cortez, Alexandria 57

Pankhurst, Emmeline 57
peer pressure 84–5, 102
Phyll, Lady 74–5
privilege 42–3, 55, 74
puberty 53–4, 108–15, 132

race 28–9, 41, 66, 71, 77
racism 41, 68–76, 121
Rana, Balwinder Singh 76
religion 18–19, 32, 36, 72, 77,
    113
respect 8, 25, 27, 37, 46–55,
    77–8, 85, 98–9, 101, 105,
    117, 151, 154
role models 21, 67
roles 15–18, 20–21, 53, 61

Sandhu, Suki 66–7
sexism 23, 41, 55–6, 74
sexual relations 24, 50–52
sexuality 30–36, 66, 77
social media 6, 46, 96, 113,
    118, 120, 147
sport 5, 23, 52, 65, 81, 120–22,
    126
Styles, Harry 21, 58–9

television 6, 32, 60, 103, 115,
    126, 130
Thomas, Gareth 31
transgender 25–7, 30, 35, 46,
    57, 58
transphobia 35, 41, 46
Trudeau, Justin 21

Velendra, Kaushik 21
Victorian era 17, 21
violence 7, 16–17, 23, 32, 41,
    45, 92–4, 95, 98, 134

Wan, Gok 116–17
Wylie, Jordan 152–4

xenophobia 68

Yousafzai, Malala 56

Acknowledgements

This book has been really important to me. It's been sitting in my brain for years trying to work its way into the world. All the lessons I've learned about how to be a better person are in here. It's one of the toughest books I have ever written because I really had to dig deep to find the words to describe what I was thinking and feeling. This is what I would have wanted to read when I was growing up and I hope that anyone who reads it finds it helpful or at the very least comforting in some way.

I couldn't have done any of it without the help and support of a wonderful bunch of people though. To Liza Wilde, Tig Wallace, Victoria Walsh, Sam Perrett, Emily Finn, Namishka Doshi, Katy Cattell and the entire team at Hachette: the biggest THANK YOU. Thanks for all your understanding, guidance and for being so patient with me! Thank you to Hamza Jahanzeb for all your wonderful comments and feedback, and to David O'Connell for bringing it all to life so beautifully.

I have to give my most heartfelt thanks to all my amazing friends who contributed their kind words and wisdom to create this book:
Jake Graf, Ryan Lanji, Emma Morris, Suki Sandhu, Charlie Christensen, Gethin Jones, Michael Gunning, Alexis Caught, Jonny Benjamin, Jordan Wylie, Lady Phyll and Gok Wan. You all inspire me so much and the world is a better place because of you.

Thank you, as always, to my friends, family and management team (KT Forster and Craig Latto) for being my support network through all of this. It's been one hell of a ride!

And last but not least, thank you to all the people who have made me who I am today and taught me everything I know about how to be me. Even though I'm a grown man, I'm still learning, but because of you I hope to be a little bit better every day.